# THE
# ENGLISH FUSEE LEVER POCKET WATCH

Its History, Development,
Service and Repair

# THE
# ENGLISH
# FUSEE LEVER
# POCKET
# WATCH

## Its History, Development, Service and Repair

## CHRISTOPHER S. BARROW

First published in 2019 by NAG Press,
an imprint of
The Crowood Press Ltd,
Ramsbury, Marlborough
Wiltshire SN8 2HR

enquiries@crowood.com

**www.crowood.com**

**British Library Cataloguing-in-Publication Data**
A catalogue record for this book is available from
the British Library.

ISBN 978 0 7198 3015 0

Typeset by Chapter One Book Production,
Knebworth, UK

Printed and bound in India by Parksons Graphics

# Contents

# List of Illustrations

## Illustrations in Appendix III

# Introduction

The aim of this book is to give an insight into the development and history of the detached lever escapement, and also to provide a detailed and comprehensive manual to guide the enthusiastic amateur through the repair and servicing of an English fusee lever pocket watch. The book also covers some of the variants of the detached lever, including the rack lever, the Massey lever (types I to V) and the Savage two-pin lever.

## The History of the Fusee Lever

The invention of the pocket watch is usually attributed to the master locksmith Peter Henlein of Nuremberg (1480–1542). He is credited with making the first watch somewhere between 1504 and 1508. The watch he made was a spring-driven verge and was probably closer to a miniature clock than what we would now think of as a pocket watch. The verge escapement had been in use in church clocks from the mid-fourteenth century and remained the only escapement available to watchmakers until the early part of the eighteenth century. The eighteenth century was a time of great scientific advancement and saw the development of a number of new watch escapements, namely the Debaufre, Duplex, cylinder and rack lever. These new escapements, along with the verge, are all known as 'frictional rest' escapements; this is because the balance is always in contact with the rest of the train and so the balance can never oscillate freely, which causes problems with accuracy and reliability. The 'holy grail' for watchmakers was to develop a 'detached' escapement, which is one where the balance can oscillate independently from the influence of the rest of the watch train.

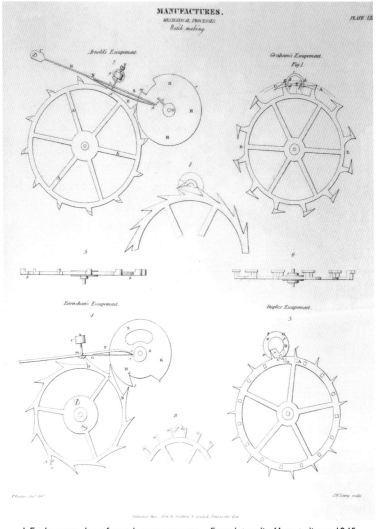

1 Early examples of watch escapements – *Encyclopeadia Metropolitana* 1845.

The question of who invented the detached lever escapement has always generated a certain amount of controversy. Both Julien Le Roy (1686–1759) and Thomas Mudge (1715–94) are credited with its invention. My view is that they both came up with the idea independently at about the same time and, therefore, the credit for the invention of the detached lever should be shared equally between them.

After the invention of the detached lever, there followed a period of experimentation, with several variations on Mudge's original design. Some of these include Emery's lever, Pendleton's lever, Leroux's layout, Ellicott's lever and Breguet's lever.

At first the detached lever escapement did not generate much interest in the watchmaking industry. In England, most watchmakers carried on using the tried and tested verge escapement and it was not until the early part of the nineteenth century that the detached lever begun to dominate the English watchmaking trade. By the mid-nineteenth century, it had become the most popular escapement used in English watches. It owes its success to the fact that it is a very reliable and robust escapement, requiring relatively little setup or adjustment, yet providing a high degree of accuracy in timekeeping.

The early nineteenth century saw a number of new versions of the detached lever escapement before finally settling on the table roller lever. Other types of detached lever escapement that survived those early days include the Massey

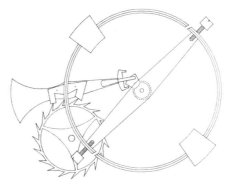

2 Drawing of an unusual escapement from a watch by James Tupman, London, 1825.

(type I to V), Savage two-pin lever and rack lever (although the latter is not detached).

## The Rack Lever

The rack lever escapement was invented by Jean d'Hautefeuille (1647–1724) in 1722 in Orléans, France. It seems to have had only limited interest from the watchmaking trade until Peter Litherland (1756–1805), working in Liverpool, developed the escapement, taking out two patents in 1791 and 1792 for a rack lever escapement. The design of the escapement consists of a conventional ratchet-toothed escape wheel and lever pallets. The end of the lever is not a fork, as with the table roller lever, but is formed of a segment of a toothed wheel or rack. The rack engages with a pinion on the balance staff. As the rack moves from side to side it causes the pinion and balance to rotate. The rack is prevented from disengaging with the balance pinion by means of the banking pins. Because the rack and pinion remains engaged at all times, it is not classified as detached.

Balance staff

3 A rack lever escapement.

In spite of the lack of detachment, the escapement still performs well and all the examples I have worked on have been of a very high standard of workmanship and run well with a good strong tick. The escapement was only ever made by watchmakers in the Liverpool region, never having been taken up by the London watch-trade.

There is some speculation that the rack lever was the forerunner of the detached lever but there is no real evidence of this being the case. Neither Mudge's nor Le Roy's escapements bear any resemblance to the rack lever. I think the rack lever was just one of many evolutionary dead-ends in the development of the detached lever escapement.

## The Massey Lever (Type I to V)

Edward Massey (1768–1852) was born in Newcastle-under-Lyme into a family that already had a high reputation as toolmakers. Edward Massey first applied for a patent in 1802 for a log and sounding machine, used by the navy, among others. In 1812, Massey patented a design for a detached lever escapement, which became known as a 'Massey type I'. A later patent for 1814 details types II to V. All five designs are variations on a theme: they consist of a steel cylinder with a projection (either formed of steel or an attached cylindrical ruby) fitted on to the balance staff. One of the major advantages of the Massey escapement is that the safety action is integral to the design (*see* the chapter 'The Lever' for a description on how the safety action functions on a table roller lever escapement). Massey was not really a watchmaker but specialized in making escapements for other watchmakers and, as a result, did not sign many watches. Massey's escapement did, however, appear in many watches and was a popular escapement until the 1850s when the table roller

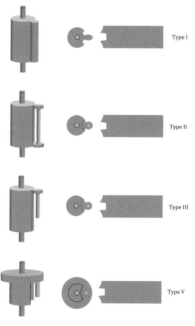

4 Massey escapements.

lever took over. For a detailed look at the Massey family *see* Alan Treherne's *Catalogue of an Exhibition at the Museum, Newcastle-under-Lyme.*

It is not clear why the Massey escapement lost out to the table roller lever. All the examples I have worked on have been well made and perform reliably, the design being simple to make and robust.

## The Savage Two-Pin Escapement

George Savage (?–1855) invented the escapement that bears his name between 1814 and 1818; he never patented the escapement. The name is, in fact, a bit of a misnomer, as it is formed of three pins. The escapement consists of a roller fitted to the balance staff, on to which are mounted two pins set either side of a small notch. The lever has a wide fork, which engages with the pins on the roller and, as they do, unlocks the escape wheel. The lever also has a pin, mounted between the arms of the fork, which engages with the notch on the roller; this pin provides most of the impulse to the balance and also the safety action.

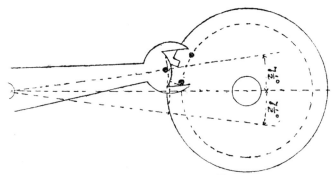

Fig. 6.  Savage's Two Pin.

5 Savage two-pin escapement from *Watch and Clockmakers' Handbook, Dictionary and Guide*, Britten 1889.

The escapement was never popular with watchmakers and, therefore, is quite rare; I have only worked on a couple of pocket watches with a Savage two-pin escapement. One reason for this may be that the pins that unlock the escape wheel are prone to wear and, in some examples, the two pins have been replaced by a single, oval-shaped jewel.

## The Demise of the English Watch Trade

Early English watchmaking (late sixteenth century and seventeenth century) required a wide range of skills on the part of the watchmaker, as they made the entire watch from scratch. Watchmakers may have brought in a few specialist parts like springs but would have handmade all other parts, including dials and cases.

By the eighteenth century, the English watch trade began to change to a system based around groups of skilled artisans, each one producing a particular part (such as wheels, pinions, chains). These parts were still mostly handmade, although as the century progressed, machines were increasingly used to make some parts. The various parts were then brought together and assembled into a basic movement known as an *ébauche*. The *ébauches* were then supplied to watchmakers who would finish the movement, fitting and adjusting the escapement, engraving the movement, fitting the dial and hands, and fitting the completed movement in its case.

By the mid-nineteenth century, the English watch trade had become pre-eminent. However, this position

6 English machine-made going barrel lever pocket watch movement.

was soon to be challenged: first, by the American machine-made watches from companies like Waltham and Elgin; later the challenge came from Swiss-made watches. There were attempts in England to set up companies making machine-made watches; one such enterprise was the Lancashire Watch Company (1889–1910), but these were ultimately unsuccessful and the international watch trade moved away from England as the nineteenth century came to a close.

## The Verge Conversion

Sooner or later you will come across this strange hybrid. Outwardly, it will probably look like a conventional verge pocket watch, but when you take a look at the movement you will soon realize that there have been changes to the original design. What you are looking at is a much-loved verge watch that the owner has decided to have updated to the latest

7 An example of a verge watch that has been converted to a lever escapement.

escapement. The way this has been carried out will depend on the individual watchmaker, but most follow a similar pattern. The balance will have been changed; the crown and contrate wheels will have been removed. A new plate will have been fitted to take the lower pivot of the balance and accommodate the new lever, escape, fourth and modified third wheels. The fusee, mainspring and centre wheel will have been retained, along with the original motion work under the dial. Because the original dial is usually kept, there is unlikely to be a second hand.

# How a Fusee Lever Works

Apocket watch is defined as a portable device for measuring and displaying the time of day and small enough to fit in a pocket. It does this by accurately controlling the release of stored energy; this energy comes from the coiled mainspring, which is connected, via a number of wheels and pinions, to the escapement. Hands are attached to the ends of some of the arbors and these are used to indicate the time (hours, minutes and seconds).

The mainspring consists of a length of spring steel wound tightly inside a barrel. The outer end of the mainspring is attached to the inside of the barrel; the inner end of the mainspring is attached to the barrel arbor, about which the barrel rotates. The barrel is connected, via the fusee chain, to the fusee, which, via the great wheel (part of the fusee), drives the rest of the train (the wheels and pinions). The train transmits the energy, stored in the mainspring, to the escapement. The ratio of the number of teeth on each wheel and pinion determines the relative rate at which each wheel rotates. The function of these wheels and pinions is to convert from the low-speed rotation of the barrel to the high-speed of rotation required at the escapement. The fusee rotates approximately once every four to six hours; the escape wheel rotates approximately once every six seconds, depending on the design of the watch.

The most important part of a watch is the escapement. This provides the means of controlling the rate at which a watch

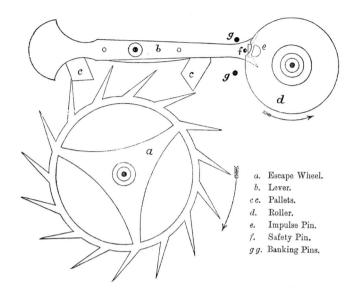

a. Escape Wheel.
b. Lever.
c c. Pallets.
d. Roller.
e. Impulse Pin.
f. Safety Pin.
g g. Banking Pins.

8 Lever escapement from *Watch and Clockmakers' Handbook, Dictionary and Guide*, Britten 1889.

runs. In a typical fusee lever watch, the balance oscillates five times per second but there are variations where the balance oscillates at different frequencies. Thomas Yeats (1812–90) of Preston, produced a number of watches where the balance only oscillates twice per second (known as a slow beat escapement).

When watching the balance on a ticking movement, it can look as if the balance is causing the lever to move backwards and forwards. However, the reverse is in fact true: the lever causes the balance to swing.

9 A lever from a typical English fusee lever escapement.

The escapement consists of the lever, one end of which is shaped like a two-pronged fork; to one side of the lever are mounted the pallets. The pallets' job is to alternatively 'lock' and 'un-lock' the teeth of the escape wheel, and in so doing, receives an impulse as the escape-wheel teeth slide along

10 A ratchet-toothed escape wheel.

the sloped edge of the pallet. With the lever at rest against one of the banking pins, as the balance rotates, the impulse jewel enters the fork and starts to move the lever away from the banking pin, and in so doing, overcomes the 'draw' (*see* next section for details). As the lever is moved further away from the banking pin, the lever pallet that was locking one of the escape wheel teeth, releases that tooth and the escape wheel rotates until the next tooth locks on the opposite lever pallet. As the freed escape wheel tooth slides against its pallet, it gives the lever a 'kick'. This kick is then transferred to the impulse jewel via the lever fork, and in so doing, imparts energy to the balance, causing it to continue rotating. When the balance reaches the end of its swing, it stops and then reverses owing to the tensioning in the balance spring. As it swings back the other way, the whole process is repeated. So each time the impulse jewel engages with the lever fork, it is given a kick and, as a result, the balance is kept in motion and the watch running. The balance is in contact with the lever for only a very short part of the time the balance is in motion, and hence the reason why this type of escapement is known as a 'detached' lever.

## Draw

One problem that became apparent with early lever watches was that, if the watch received a sharp knock, the lever could move before the balance was in the right position to receive its impulse. If this happens, the lever could interfere with the free swing of the balance. To overcome this problem, the slope on the lever pallets was adjusted so that the escape wheel teeth are positively 'drawn' into position after locking. This causes a small amount of recoil in the train, but this is more than offset by the advantage gained by keeping the lever in position between impulse cycles.

# Tools

The complete list of tools shown below could be seen as an ideal list; it is possible to clean and carry out basic repairs with a reduced set of tools. It is probably better to only buy a basic set of tools to start with, and then purchase the others as and when you need them. Most of the basic tools would be readily available (*see* Appendix I), but the specialized ones may prove to be a little more difficult to obtain. It is always worth keeping an eye out on auction sites or antique fairs for second-hand tools, especially the ones that are no longer made.

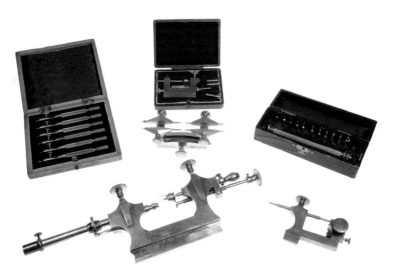

II A selection of antique pocket watch tools.

It is good practice to buy the highest quality tools you can afford. Cheap ones will often perform less well and may even cause damage to the watch. One of the best makers of watch tools is Bergeon. This Swiss company produces a huge range of tools and materials specially designed for the watch repairer. They are not cheap, but will repay the initial cost by giving years of good and reliable service.

In the following list of tools, those marked with an * are the ones I consider essential to start watch repair work.

- Arkansas stone.
- Blower for removing dust.*
- Round or smoothing broaches (burnisher).
- Case knife.*
- Craft knife with retractable blade.*
- Cutters (strong enough to cut steel).*
- Light source (good quality and adjustable).*
- Glue.*
- Hammer (brass faced).
- Hand lifter.*
- Hand-fitting tool.*
- Heat source (spirit lamp or gas stove).
- Jacot tool.
- Jeweller's hammer.*
- Magnifying glass and eye pieces (if you wear glasses, you might consider a clip-on one) X3 and X10.*
- Metal polish (brass/gold and silver).*
- Movement holder.*
- Needle files.*

- Nylon brush with retractable bristles for removing rust, etc.
- Oil pot.*
- Oilers.*
- Pliers (brass-faced).*
- Pliers (flat-faced).*
- Peg wood.*
- Pin vice.*
- Pith wood.*
- Cutting broaches (reamer).
- Rubber work mat.*
- Screwdrivers (0.8mm to 4mm) ideally with replaceable blades. For ease of use, it might be worth looking for a set, which is stored in a rotating storage base.*
- Screwdriver sharpening tool used to hold the screwdriver at a fixed angle to the stone.
- Solvent cleaner.*
- Storage tray, segmented with lid.*
- Sharpening stone (diamond impregnated type).
- Staking tool and punches.
- Steel wool (0000 grade).
- Tapered pins (brass and nickel).*
- Taps and dies.
- Tweezers (anti-magnetic).*
- Un-sterilized surgical gloves.*
- Watch keys (No. 00 to No. 12).*
- Watch oil (Moebius 8000 or similar high-grade synthetic oil).*
- Wire in a range of sizes (brass and steel).

12 A staking tool in fitted box with a range of punches.

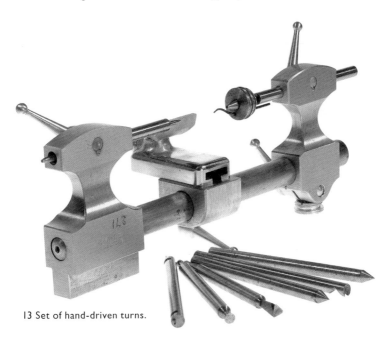

13 Set of hand-driven turns.

## Tool Maintenance

It is good practice to maintain all your tools in top condition. This makes them easier to use and less likely to cause damage to a watch or movement. If any become broken or worn, they should be replaced or repaired.

Try to get into the habit of cleaning tools like tweezers and screwdrivers regularly by pushing them into a piece of pith wood – this will remove dirt and oil.

### Screwdrivers

Always maintain a good, sharp blade, as this will prevent damage to the screw head. Use a screwdriver holder and stone; fit the screwdriver in the holder, and check that the blade forms the same angle with the stone as the current angle of the blade and that it is square on to the stone. Run the holder backwards and forwards a few times and then check the blade with a loupe. When you are happy, turn it over and repeat for the other side. Finally, use an Arkansas stone across the end of the blade to produce a flat, square end.

14 A screwdriver being sharpened.

## Tweezers

For these to work properly, the ends need to meet at the tip. Rub an Arkansas stone over the internal faces of the tweezers to makes sure they are smooth, and run the stone over the points to keep them sharp.

## Pliers

Again, the internal faces need to be smooth and parallel. Use an Arkansas stone to smooth the internal faces.

# Preparation

It is important to arrange your workplace before starting on any watch. Make sure your workbench is clear (try not to start more than one watch at a time, although this does sometime happen!). Make sure that you are seated at a comfortable level to the desk and that you have enough free space to work in. Pay particular attention to the lighting; a good movable lamp is essential. A good-quality LED 'daylight' lamp gives the best sort of working light; ideally the lamp should be able to move into any position, including the ability to rotate the head. Make sure the work area is clean and free from dust. The use a specially designed rubber mat will help to prevent parts from rolling off the desk and also protects the surface of the desk.

If you are not that familiar with the workings of a pocket watch, it might be worth taking a few photos or making sketches during the dismantling process. These will prove to be invaluable when you come to reassemble the watch.

It is very important to use the right size of screwdriver. This means the blade width should be the same as the width of the screw head (note that because the screw head may not have parallel sides, it is the width at the bottom of the slot that is important). If the screwdriver blade is wider than the screw head, there is a risk of it catching on the surrounding metal and damaging this; if smaller, there is a risk of damaging the screw slot. The blade should also be the correct thickness so that it forms a tight fit in the slot.

This is probably a good time to mention a particular problem when working on watches, which is that there are quite a few parts whose aim in life is to fly off at an odd angle and hide themselves (I'm convinced that some of them grow legs as they fly through the air, so when they land on the floor, they can run under any item of furniture and hide). This means hours spent on your hands and knees trying to find some vital part. There is not an easy way to avoid this problem other than to be aware that as you dismantle a watch, some parts are likely to fly off if you are not careful.

A word of warning: when you obtain a watch, even if it looks to be in good condition, do not be tempted to wind it up until you have dismantled, cleaned and oiled it. This is because there is a very real chance that parts will have seized up owing to the old oil drying out; this is especially true for the mainspring, which may break if put under strain after having been allowed to dry out.

## Care with Handling Watches

Always work over a bench or desk when handling a watch; ideally cover the surface with a soft material, such as paper or a rubber mat, so that if you are unfortunate enough to drop a watch or movement, you are less likely to damage it.

It is good practice to wear some form of protective gloves when handling a watch movement; un-sterilized surgical gloves are good as they are thin enough to still allow you to feel the parts. These will help prevent the possibility of contamination from the natural oils on your skin, which can leave permanent fingerprints etched into the surface of some parts, particularly if they are made of steel.

Once a watch movement has been removed from its case, great care must be taken to prevent damage to parts that protrude (cannon pinion, fourth wheel pivot and so on). Never put pressure on a movement while it is lying on the bench, always support the movement by the edge. The safest way to achieve this is to use a movement holder, which supports the movement in an adjustable frame.

Remember always to check whether there is tension in the mainspring before removing any parts. There is a large amount of energy stored in a fully wound mainspring and if released in an uncontrolled way, it could cause serious damage to the movement or, worse still, the watch repairer!

15 A fusee lever watch movement in a holder.

## Handling Parts

Most of the parts in a pocket watch are made of either brass or steel and appropriate care is required in handling both materials. Most of the steel parts (pinion, pivots and so on) will probably have been hardened to some extent by heating them up to a particular temperature and then cooling them rapidly. This makes the parts very hard and so resistant to wear, but this process also makes them more brittle. So, when handling steel parts, be careful not to bend them; this is particularly true of pivots, which can so easily be broken if subjected to a sideways force when removing them from pivot holes, for example.

Brass is a much softer material then steel and, therefore, is not so likely to be damaged if bent (it can usually be returned to its original shape). The problem with brass parts, such as wheels, is that, if they are not handled with care, they can become distorted, preventing them from engaging correctly with the next wheel's pinion.

## Dust Removal

During handling and assembly of a watch movement and parts, do not be tempted to blow dust away, as your breath is damp and could cause problems with corrosion, particularly on parts made of steel. Always use a blower special designed for the job of dust removal.

## Oil

This is probably one of the most contentious issues in the watch repair world. If you ask ten watchmakers what kind of oil to use, you will get ten different answers.

A lot of modern oils sold by watch material supplies are too light for pocket watches, as they are designed for wristwatches. The requirement for good pocket watch oil is that it is pure, so never be tempted to buy cheap oil as this probably contains impurities, which will cause problems with corrosion, etc. When oiling a watch, it is best practice to apply light oil to those parts that are subject to low torque/high speed (i.e. fourth wheel, escape wheel, lever and balance) and heavier oil to those parts that are subjected to high torque/low speed (i.e. third wheel, centre wheel and fusee). That said, if the reason for restoration is to have a working watch that will probably only be run once every few months, then you can use the same high-grade oil throughout the watch.

Moebius, a Swiss company who have been making oils for the watch and clock industry for many years, makes a range of very high-quality synthetic oils designed for different uses. Their 8000 watch oil should provide all your lubrication requirements.

### How and Where to Oil

Never take oil directly from the glass vial that the oil is stored in as it is very easy for the oil to become contaminated; instead, transfer a small drop to an oil storage box, which is a small, round container about 30mm in diameter with a tight-fitting lid. In the centre of the cup is a depression into which a drop of oil is introduced. The lid should be kept on when not in use so as to avoid dust and dirt from contaminating the oil.

When applying oil to pivots, it is very important not to over oil; this is because the excess oil can find its way to parts that should not be oiled and cause problems. Also, oil has a habit of attracting dust, which then forms itself into a sticky mess that, over time, will affect the running of the watch. The rule of thumb is that if you can see the oil on the pivot, you have put too much on. If you do put too much oil on a pivot, use a small piece of paper towel to absorb the excess. When applying oil, use an oil pin, which is a tool consisting of a handle with a piece of thin wire whose end has been flattened and then sharped to a point. They come in different sizes, depending on how much oil is required to be delivered. Take the oil pin and dip it into the oil pot, then transfer the oil to the pivot by touching the end of the oil pin on the pivot; the correct amount of oil will then be delivered. Repeat for all pivots. The surfaces of the lever pallets, which act on the escape wheel, should also be smeared with a very small amount of oil. Also, remember to oil the centre wheel arbor (where it passes through the top plate) before you fit the cannon pinion.

# Where to Obtain Watches

The watches I repair have been obtained from a number of sources; this list may be helpful in your own search:

- Antique shops (you may have to ask whether they have any broken watches, as these are not normally on display).
- Second-hand, junk and charity shops.
- On-line auctions.
- Traditional auction houses.
- Antique and collectors' fairs.
- Specialist watch and clock fairs.
- Your own family and friends.

Once the word gets out that you repair watches, people will be beating a path to your door. However, be careful if you do take on watches from friends or family, make sure that you are either fully capable of repairing these or that they accept the consequences of the watch being returned in a less than perfect condition! It is probably better to practise on watches you have brought yourself before tackling those from friends and family.

In buying a watch to repair, first consider its potential – how much work will it need? Broken pivots, especially the balance pivots, are more difficult to repair than a broken mainspring. Look at the overall condition of the movement: missing screws,

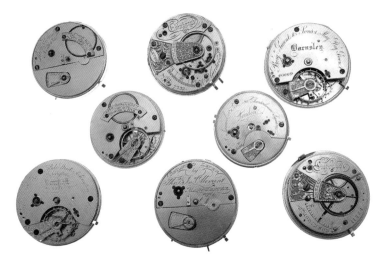

16 A selection of nineteenth century full, three-quarter and half plate movements.

for example, may indicate that someone has attempted to repair the watch before. Check that all the parts are present, as it may not be possible to find replacement parts. Does the movement fit the case? It is not uncommon to find a movement that has been re-housed!

## The Past Life of a Watch

What might have happened before you become the owner of a watch? The chances are that when you obtain a watch, from whatever source, you have no way of knowing what might have happened to it during its long life. The watch may have simply stopped due to the oil drying out and been put aside with the intention of taking it to the watch repairer, in which case it is a fairly straightforward process to bring the watch back to working order. However, a lot more may have happened along the way. Common faults are broken parts, particularly pivots, mainsprings and fusee chains. The watch may not work because a replacement part is the wrong size, such as a wheel, or it may be that a replacement screw is too long and interfering with other parts. Parts may have been glued together to effect a repair (not good practice).

For this reason, always be sceptical about the state of any pocket watch until you have had a chance to dismantle it and examine every part. It is also best not to wind a newly acquired pocket watch until it has been examined and cleaned.

# Winding a Watch

An English fusee lever pocket watch is almost always wound anticlockwise and from the rear. It is not uncommon to come across front-wind verge pocket watches, usually in full hunter cases, but very rare for fusee lever pocket watches to be front wind (I have never personally come across one). To wind a watch, place the key over the winding square and give it four to six full turns of the key, until you hit a firm 'stop'. It is very important that you do not try to force the key any further, as this will almost certainly cause damage to the watch.

## Over-Wound

'Over-wound' is a common fault attributed to a watch that is not working. It is almost always an incorrect diagnosis, as it is usually applied to a watch that is fully wound but not running. It is, in fact, quite difficult, but not impossible, to truly over-wind a pocket watch (go past the point when the mainspring is fully wound). With a fusee watch, this means continuing to wind after the 'stop' has engaged. If you do this, you will soon run out of fusee chain and the chain will either disengage from the barrel or the chain will break. This will lead to a very rapid unwinding of the mainspring and a characteristic 'whizz' as the barrel spins round at high speed.

## Setting the Hands

Almost all English fusee lever pocket watches have their hands set by a key (there are a few examples of 'keyless' hand setting but these are very rare in watches dating before the 1890s). For front-set hands, a key (usually the same key that is used to wind the watch) is placed over the square section at the top

of the cannon pinion, where the hands meet, and rotated until the hands are set to the correct time; the hands can be rotated in either direction. Under no circumstances should you be tempted to move the hands directly by pushing them round.

17 Setting the hands on a front-set watch.

For rear-set hands, the process is the same except the key is placed over the rear set hands square.

18 Setting the hands on a rear-set watch.

41

# Dials

19 A typical example of a mid-nineteenth century enamel dial.

The vast majority of dials found on an English fusee lever pocket watch are made of vitreous enamel (sometimes erroneously referred to as porcelain). A dial is made of a disc of copper, on to which the dial feet have been soldered. A layer of enamel mixed with metallic oxides is then fused on to the copper disc using a high-temperature furnace. The type of metallic oxide added to the enamel determines the colour of the dial, which usually ranges from a strong blue tint through white to cream.

The enamel produces a very hard, smooth surface, which does not fade or discolour with time. The numerals and other decoration are then painted on by hand and the dial fired again to fuse these into the enamel. The major drawback with enamelled dials is that they are prone to damage if the watch is dropped or mishandled (either producing chips or hairline cracks).

Other materials used for dials are silver, gold and, in very low-quality watches, paper.

20 Underside of a dial showing the dial foot.

## Cleaning Dials

Before trying anything more complicated, give the dial a clean with soap and warm water (not too hot, as this could damage the enamel, particularly if it already has hairline cracks). After cleaning, dry it off with a paper towel. If the dial has hairline cracks, these can sometimes be made to look less obvious by soaking in a mild bathroom cleaner (Bath Power by OzKlee or similar works well). The numerals are almost always fused on to the dial and, therefore, unlikely to be removed by any cleaning. However, if there is other writing or painting on the dial (e.g. maker's name), care must be exercised to make sure that this is not removed during cleaning, so check a small area first. Once the dial has been cleaned, put it safely to one side.

The subsidiary seconds dial is often made separately from the main dial (usual if the subsidiary seconds dial is sunken) and held in place with glue, shellac or soldered in place. Be aware that it is possible that the subsidiary seconds dial can sometimes come loose during the cleaning process. If this happens you will need to fix it back in place. First, carefully remove any of the old fixing, applying as little pressure as possible to the enamel rim on the dial, as this is very easily damaged. When all the old fixing has been removed, place the subsidiary seconds dial in place and check that the '30' is aligned with the 6 o'clock position, and hold in place with a piece of masking tape across the front of the main and subsidiary dials. Double check that all is still aligned and the subsidiary dial is level with respect to the main dial, then apply soft glue (one that does not dry completely hard) around the junction between the two dials. Leave aside until the glue has set, then clean away any excess glue with a craft knife.

## Repairing Dials

It is not an easy or straightforward process to repair an enamel dial; there is, however, a kit 'Curator Enamel & Porcelain Dial Repair Kit' (obtainable from Walsh, Cousins, and others; *see* Appendix I for details) that can be used to repair most problems. It contains clear epoxy resin, pigments to colour the resin and ink to re-paint the numerals, plus full instructions. By using the kit, it is possible to make a reasonable job of repairing even a quite badly damaged dial.

## Brass-Tapered Pins

Whether used to fix the dial, dial plate, movement or balance spring in place, you will quickly become aware of the small brass pins that are used for these jobs. It is still possible to purchase these from watch material suppliers, and particularly for those used to hold the balance spring in place, it is probably best to buy these readymade. As for those used to hold the dial, etc., it is straightforward to make your own. Take a length of brass wire about 2cm long and just greater in diameter than the hole through which it is to be inserted. Hold the brass rod tightly in a pin vice with approximately 1 cm protruding. Place the end of the brass rod on the surface of a stone and at a very slight angle to the surface of the stone. Then, while continually rotating the pin vice between your thumb and finger, rub the brass rod backwards and forward along the stone until a suitable pin is formed. Remove the brass rod from the pin vice and cut off the waste to leave a tapered pin.

# Dust Caps

Most English fusee lever pocket watches are fitted with a dust cap – a brass cover that fits over the movement and whose function is to keep dust and pocket fluff from getting into the movement. There are three basic types:

- A brass cover that completely covers the movement, with a cut-out for the balance cock, and held in place by a sliding steel clip.

21 Standard dust cap.

- A brass ring, known as a rim dust cap, that covers the gap between the top plate and bottom plate, and is held in place by two screws in the top plate.

22 An example of a rim dust cap.

- A brass cover hinged on one side with a spring that flips it open when a catch is pressed. More usually found on three-quarter or half-plate movements.

23 Spring-load dust cap with catch.

If a dust cap is missing it is quite difficult to replace it, as each one was handmade to fit a particular movement. You may be lucky and find one that is the same size as the original, but this will be rare.

A common fault is that the sliding steel clip breaks; it is sometimes possible to replace this with one from another dust cap. The replacement needs to be the same length and have the same curvature as the original one. If you are lucky, the small projection on the clip, which locks and unlocks the cap, is a small screw, in which case all you need to do is unscrew it and the clip can be slid over until it disengages from the cap. If it is not a screw, then you need to carefully lift up the clip near the centre with a piece of peg wood and slide it over until it disengages (do not lift too much as there is a risk of breaking the clip). Remove the broken clip from the dust cap and fit the replacement one, making sure it can move freely.

# Jewelling

Jewelling in English pocket watches was introduced around the start of the eighteenth century, as a means of reducing the wear between the pivot and pivot hole. Because of the high cost of providing jewelling in the eighteenth century, it was only used in very high-quality watches. It was not until the nineteenth century that it became more commonplace.

24 Full plate fusee lever movement with 'Liverpool' jewelling.

An English fusee lever movement usually has a minimum of seven jewels: balance (four jewels, top and bottom pivots both with jewelled end caps), impulse jewel and lever pallets. It can, however, have up to twenty-three jewels: balance, impulse pin, lever pallets, lever pivots, escape (capped), fourth, third, centre wheel pivots and the fusee.

You might occasionally come across a watch movement with over-sized jewels on the top plate; these are commonly known as 'Liverpool jewelling'. They have no additional function but were employed to make the movement look more attractive to the potential buyer (note that the corresponding pivot in the bottom plate is of a normal size).

The jewels used in an English fusee lever are almost always mounted in brass or gold mounts, which are then held in place by screws. This means that if a jewel is damaged, it is a fairly straightforward job to replace it by substituting one from another movement.

# Cases

The fusee lever pocket watch can be found in five basic watchcase styles, these are:

- **Pair Case** – although the pair case is usually associated with verge pocket watches, you will come across quite a few examples of fusee lever movement fitted into a pair case. These cases are original to the movement.

25 Pair case pocket watch.

- **Double-Bottomed Open Face** – the most common case style for the fusee lever. This has a front bezel, usually hinged at 9 o'clock and opened via a lug at 2 o'clock. The rear cover is opened by pressing the pendant button, which releases the catch, and the cover then flips open due to the cover spring. A simpler variation has a

26 A double-bottomed pocket watchcase.

design that omits the cover spring and catch: the cover is opened via a lug at the edge of the rear cover, to the right of the pendant.

- **Double-Bottomed Full Hunter** – constructed in a similar way to the double-bottomed open face case but with the addition of a metal front cover over the bezel and watch glass. The aim of this is to protect the watch glass while in the pocket. The front cover flips open when the pendant button is pressed. Because the front cover completely covers the inner bezel and watch glass, the front cover needs to be opened in order to read the time. The rear cover is usually opened via a lug to the right of the pendant. Very occasionally you might come across a case with a split pendant button: one half opening the front cover and the other half opening the rear cover.

27 Full hunter pocket watch.

- **Double-Bottomed Half Hunter** – a variation on the full hunter case but with the addition of a small, glazed window in the centre of the front cover that allows the time to be read without opening the front cover.

28 Half hunter pocket watch.

51

- **Double-Backed** – this design has an inner and outer rear cover, both hinged at 6 o'clock, and is most commonly associated with the centre second chronograph but is also used with other half and three-quarter plate movements. As with the double-bottomed case, the front bezel opens via a lug at 2 o'clock. The rear outer cover also opens via a lug to the right of the pendant; this usually gives you access to the winding square and hand setting square. The inner cover is opened using a case knife inserted into the small indent at 1 o'clock; this gives access to the rear of the movement.

29 Double-backed pocket watch.

English makers from the early nineteenth century favoured the double-bottomed case for full plate movements. It was not possible with this design of case to access the movement from the rear; this could only be accessed from the front by opening the front bezel and unclipping the movement via the catch at 6 o'clock. The movement could then be lifted up on the hinge at 12 o'clock (the movement is usually covered by a dust cap).

## Case Repairs

I should start by saying that, in general, case repairs are quite difficult, particularly if they involve soldering. As with most watch repairs, it is better to practise on old and damaged cases before moving on to good ones.

Before starting any repair work on a case, consider whether

it might be better to leave the problem alone and live with the imperfection rather than risk doing more damage trying to repair it.

Small dents and bumps can usually be removed from gold and silver cases without too much trouble. Place the case, with the raised part of the bump uppermost, on a firm but soft surface (a piece of thick rubber works well). Then, using a jeweller's hammer, lightly tap the area until the bump is as flat as it can be made. It is a good idea to protect the area you are hammering with something like masking tape to reduce the risk of marking it.

The same method can be tried on gold-plated cases but be careful because the thin layer of gold can easily be damaged. Also, note that the base metal is usually brass, which is harder than gold or silver and, therefore, it is more difficult to remove dents.

The pin that forms the hinge on cases can sometimes break. To replace this you first need to remove the broken pin, which can be tricky. If the two parts of the case can be separated, it is usually easier to work from the inside of the hinge. Use a short length of steel wire, just smaller in diameter than the hinge pin, and place it on the end of the old hinge pin, tapping the end of the wire with a hammer. This should push the old bit of the hinge pin out. If the broken pin proves to be stubborn, try soaking the area overnight in WD40 or releasing oil. Once the broken pieces of the hinge pin have been removed, assemble the parts of the case and using a cutting broach, very carefully clean the inside of the tube where the hinge pin goes (just a couple of turns of the broach should be enough). Then take a new tapered nickel pin of a suitable size and push it into the tube until it is firmly in place. Try the parts of the case to make sure they open and close correctly. Mark the points on the pin where it enters and exits the hinge tubes, then withdraw the pin and cut off the excess. File both ends smooth and at an angle so that when the pin is re-inserted, the ends of the new pin are aligned with the sloping ends of the hinge tubes. Finally, clean the ends with grade 0000 wire wool. Push the pin back into the hinge tube and you should now have a working hinge.

## Making a New Pendant Button

The pendant button is held in place by the bow screw, which also holds the bow in place. The bow screw often goes missing or breaks, and this may lead to the pendant button falling out. You may be lucky and have a spare one that will fit but more often than not you will need to make a replacement.

Take a length of brass rod just slightly smaller than the hole where the pendant button fits: this will form the button. Then take a length of brass rod about 15mm long with a diameter that allows it to fit into the smaller hole in the pendant (you should be able to press down on the rear cover catch and open the rear cover). Drill a hole in the centre of the larger piece of rod that is just slightly smaller than the 15mm length of rod to a depth of about 5mm. The drilled end of the button then needs to be shaped with a file so that it fits the inside of the pendant. Tap the smaller rod into the button until it reaches the end of the drilled hole. You may need to file a very slight taper onto one end of the smaller rod (before it is inserted) in order that it fits the hole in the button. Try the new button to see if it works. You will probably find that the smaller rod is too long, so with cutters remove small amounts until the correct length is reached. The correct length is one that lets you push the button in enough to release the catch before the button reaches the bottom of the inside of the pendant. Once you are happy that the assembly works, place it in the pendant as far as it goes (without pressing on it) and mark the position of the hole in the pendant where the bow screw goes. Withdraw the new pendant button and dill a hole through the centre at the marked position of the bow screw. This hole will need to be enlarged and elongated, so that when the pendant button is in position, the hole is large enough for the bow screw to pass through the button assembly and still allow the button to be pressed down to release the rear cover. When this is done, place the button assembly back into the pendant and, with no pressure on the button, mark the top of the pendant on the button. Remove the new pendant button and about 1–2mm above this mark, cut the remainder of the rod off. With the assembly held in a vice, smooth off the top and round off the edge of the button, then finish with 0000 grade steel wool. If you want the button to match the watchcase, this can be done by rubbing the button with silver-plating solution. The finished button assembly should look as illustrated.

| 30 A pendant button and brass rods used to make a replacement. | 31 Finished replacement pendant button. |

## How a Movement is Fixed in a Case

With double-bottomed cases, the movement is almost always held in the case by a spring-loaded catch at 6 o'clock. This consists of a shaped piece of metal fitted at the edge of the bottom plate, which can move in when pressed. The catch is held proud of the bottom plate by a spring.

32 Movement catch, note underside of movement has not been gilded.

The method of holding the movement in place (with one or two exceptions) is also used for pair case, full and half hunter watches.

Centre second chronograph watches are usually housed in a double-backed case. The method used to fix the movement in place can at first sight look like that used for double-bottomed cases. The difference is that they do not make use of a spring-loaded catch but instead are held at the 6 o'clock position by a brass pin, about 1–2mm in diameter, which protrudes from the edge of the bottom plate and engages with a hole on the inside rim of the case. The 'hinge' at 12 o'clock is held in place with a brass pin. Because the top fitting looks like a hinge, it is quite common to find that someone has forced the bottom (6 o'clock) fixing thinking that the movement is designed to hinge up at 12 o'clock. If you are lucky, you will only need to replace the pin.

A much less common method of fixing the movement into the case is to use screws that pass through the case from the rear, with the heads of the screws overlapping the movement. This sometimes turns up on half and three-quarter plate watches throughout the nineteenth century.

# The Fusee

The fusee was well known and documented from the early 1400s and seems to have been introduced into clocks at about the same time as the mainspring. A clock dating from the 1430s, made for Philip the Good, Duke of Burgundy (1396–1467), is the earliest surviving example of a spring-driven clock incorporating a fusee. Leonardo da Vinci (1452–1519) sketched a machine, which includes a fusee, in 1490, as did Fillippo Brunelleschi (1377–1446), the great Italian Renaissance architect and engineer.

The word 'fusee' derives from the French and Latin word '*fusata*' meaning a spindle full of thread.

The fusee consists of a cone (strictly speaking it is a

33 Fusee chain fully wound onto the fusee.

hyperboloid) with a helical groove cut into its surface. The fusee is connected to the barrel via a fusee chain, wound round the barrel. When the watch is wound up, the chain is unwound from the barrel (tensioning the mainspring) and wound onto the fusee.

As the watch runs down, the chain unwinds from the fusee cone and returns to the barrel. This means that the torque applied via the chain acts at an increasingly greater distance from the centre of the fusee (owing to its shape), so the torque applied increases. This increase in torque offsets the reduction in the energy stored in the mainspring as it unwinds. Because springs, up until the late eighteenth century, were handmade, they each had their own individual characteristics

34 Fusee chain unwound from fusee on to barrel.

35 Side view of fusee chain as it unwinds from the barrel onto the fusee.

and, as a consequence, each fusee needed to be cut to match a particular spring.

The standard fusee, fitted to most English pocket watches, consist of five separate parts, these are:

- The fusee, including the winding square, fusee cap and fusee ratchet wheel.
- The great wheel, which is usually made of brass.
- The steel maintaining-power wheel, which incorporates the ratchet clicks.
- The maintaining-power spring.
- The fusee collet, which holds the fusee assembly together.

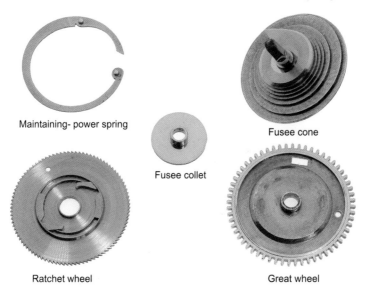

Maintaining- power spring

Fusee cone

Fusee collet

Ratchet wheel

Great wheel

36 Dismantled fusee showing the separate parts.

## Stop Work

Additional to the fusee, but associated with it, is the fusee stop work. As the watch is wound up, the fusee chain is transferred

37 Fusee stop iron.

from the barrel to the fusee and the chain rises up as it follows the groove cut in the fusee. When it reaches the top of the fusee, it engages with the stop iron.

The stop iron comprises a pivoted blued steel bar held away from the underside of the bottom plate by a weak spring. As the fusee chain reaches the top of the fusee, it pushes the stop work up until it is flush with the underside of the bottom plate. The end of the stop iron is squared off and is designed to engage with the fusee cap spur that protrudes from the top of the fusee. When the spur hits the end of the stop iron, the fusee is prevented from turning any further and the watch is said to be fully wound.

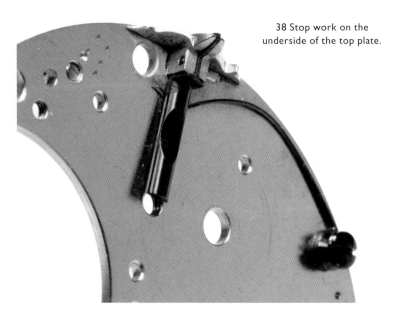

38 Stop work on the underside of the top plate.

## Common Faults with the Stop Work

- Broken or weak stop work spring.
- Bent or distorted stop iron, preventing it from engaging with the spur on the fusee.
- Misaligned fusee spur.
- Sticking stop work.

A broken or weak stop work spring can be replaced with one from an old movement. The spring needs to be long enough to fit under the stop iron but not to protrude much beyond the edge of the stop iron. If the spring protrudes too much, it runs the risk of being caught between the bottom plate and pillar, thereby preventing it from returning the stop to its correct position. This problem manifests itself when winding the watch by either the stop engaging too early or not at all, depending on which way up the movement is held.

A bent or distorted stop iron can usually be carefully adjusted back into its correct position. When fitted correctly, including the stop work spring, the end of the stop should be held away from the bottom plate sufficiently so that when the fusee is rotated, the spur can pass underneath the stop iron. If there is not enough clearance under the stop, remove the stop and, using pliers, carefully bend the end up. Only adjust by a small amount and re-fit the stop and test for clearance.

The stop iron also needs to be correctly aligned left to right. If the stop is too far left, it may catch on the raised edge of the bottom plate. If the stop is too far right, it may interfere with the fusee itself. In both cases, the stop iron can be carefully realigned by pushing it in the opposite direction, but be aware that it is all too easy to bend the stop too much and cause it to snap off, so only make small adjustments each time.

## Maintaining Power

When a fusee watch is wound, the force that is normally applied to the train by the mainspring is temporally removed. This is because the force applied by winding the watch is in the opposite direction to that applied to the train by the main-spring. This reduction in the force applied to the train has the effect of causing the watch to slow slightly. To overcome this problem, an additional flat spring is incorporated between the fusee maintaining-power wheel and the great wheel. This spring is fixed at one end to the great wheel and at the other end to the fusee maintaining-power wheel. The outer edge of the fusee maintaining-power wheel has a series of fine teeth, which engage with the fusee detent. Under normal conditions, the maintaining-power spring is kept under tension by the mainspring. As the watch is wound, the driving force from the mainspring is temporally removed from the train but the watch is kept running by the small amount of tension in the maintain-power spring.

## Fusee Repairs

### Dismantling a Fusee

To dismantle a fusee, first push out the small pin that passes through the locking washer on the underside; always apply pressure from the narrower end of the pin. The pin may be stiff and so you might need to use a length of blued steel with a point formed at one end, to push the pin out. It helps to support the fusee while you remove the pin. There are no commercially available supports, so you will need to make one out of wood. Two pieces of wood with 'V'-shaped holes mounted on a base should do the job. Once the pin has been pushed out, the locking washer can be removed, followed by the great wheel and, finally, the steel maintaining-power wheel. The maintaining spring can be removed by applying pressure to the fixing pin from the underside of the great wheel. As you dismantle the fusee, be careful not to lose any parts that have become detached, such as the ratchet clicks or ratchet wheel. Place all the parts in a tray ready for cleaning.

## Cleaning a Fusee

Place all the parts in solvent and allow them to soak, then remove and dry them with paper towel. You may need to use a brush to remove the more stubborn dirt, particularly around the ratchet clicks (be careful not to dislodge the clicks), the ratchet and the groove in which the fusee chain runs. Run a piece of sharpened peg wood around the fusee groove to clear out any stubborn dirt.

## Broken Maintaining-Power Spring

A common problem is that the maintaining spring breaks and the only thing that can be done is to replace it. Hopefully, you can use one from an old fusee of a similar size. If it is not possible to find a replacement, then you need to make one. You will need a piece of steel; a washer might provide a suitable starting point (it needs to be very slightly thicker than the original). First, file the outer curve to fit the great wheel. Then reduce the inner dimension

39 Fusee maintaining-power spring.

40 Great wheel with maintaining-power spring fitted.

to match the original spring. Remove a section of the ring, so that it has the same length as the original spring. Using a stone, reduce the thickness of the spring until it fits flush in the groove of the great wheel (as the original spring did). You now need to drill two holes approximately 1mm in diameter, one at either end to take the steel pins. Take a length of steel wire and, using a stone, taper the end so it passes through the right-hand hole. Cut off most of the wire on both sides and place on a staking tool with the pin over a suitable hole, and then, using a stake, tap the pin home. Stone the top flush with the spring and then stone the protruding end of the pin until its end is flush with the bottom of the great wheel when fitted in its final position. Repeat for the left-hand pin, only this time leave enough protruding on the top to engage with the hole in the maintaining-power wheel.

### Problems with the Ratchet Wheel

41 Underside of fusee showing ratchet wheel.

The ratchet wheel can sometimes come loose; they are usually held in place by two brass pins that are knocked into the body of the fusee. First, try placing the fusee on a staking tool and, using a flat-ended punch, tap the ratchet wheel back into place. If the pins are not a tight enough fit to stay in place, you will need to replace them. Cut two lengths of brass wire whose diameter is just slightly greater than the diameter of the fixing holes and about 5mm long. Very slightly taper the ends and then, using a flat-ended punch, tap them through the ratchet and into the body of the fusee. Cut off any excess wire and, using an Arkansas stone, smooth the ends down until flush with the ratchet.

The teeth of the ratchet may have become worn with use. This may require the replacement of the ratchet or sometimes lifting the ratchet up by a fraction of a millimetre or so can cure the problem. If the teeth are only worn on the top surface, use a craft knife to carefully lift up the ratchet wheel from the fusee. This will either bring the two fixing pins with the ratchet or leave them behind. If the fixing pins do not come away with the ratchet, use a pair of cutters to try and pull them out. If this fails, you will need to drill out the old pins. Once the ratchet is free, cut a disc from a sheet of brass 0.2mm or so thick. Place this under the ratchet and mark where the fixing and centre holes are and then drill these out. Place the disc under the ratchet and fix in place as detailed above for a loose ratchet. If the teeth are too badly damaged, you will need to fit a replacement ratchet. This can either be handmade or taken from an old broken fusee and fitted as described above.

### Problems with the Ratchet Click

The ratchet, fitted to the under-side of the fusee, engages with the ratchet clicks mounted on the maintaining-power wheel. Sometimes the ratchet clicks will be broken or bent backwards due to someone winding the watch the wrong way. The simplest solution

42 Steel ratchet wheel showing clicks.

is to replace the maintaining-power wheel with a good one from another fusee. For this to work, the replacement wheel needs to be the same diameter as the original and of a similar thickness. The ratchet wheel also needs to engage correctly with the clicks. You may need to open out the centre hole in the new maintaining-power wheel for it to fit over the central raised ring on the great wheel.

If it is not possible to find a suitable replacement maintaining-power wheel, it might be possible to replace the damaged clicks with ones taken from a scrap fusee. Place the maintaining-power wheel, with the damaged clicks, on a staking tool (clicks facing downwards), over a hole slightly bigger than the click. Using a flat-ended punch, whose diameter is just smaller than the riveted end of the click, tap the click free of the maintaining-power wheel.

43 Removing a damaged click from the steel ratchet wheel.

Repeat this process to remove the replacement click. Place the maintaining-power wheel to be repaired, face up. Fit the new click in place and, using a flat-ended punch, tap it into place. Turn the maintaining-power wheel over and, with the flat-ended punch, lightly tap the rivet. Check that the click can freely move against the spring.

44 Fixing a new click to the steel ratchet wheel.

### Reassembling a Fusee

Fit the maintaining spring into the great wheel, making sure the location pin on the underside of the spring engages with the hole on the great wheel, and then press the spring into place;

it should be flush with the surface when correctly fitted. Put a small amount of oil on the surface of the great wheel and maintaining spring. Fit the steel ratchet wheel, making sure that the pin on the maintaining spring engages with the hole in the steel ratchet wheel. Apply a small amount of oil to the ratchet clicks and on the outer surface of the steel ratchet wheel. Fit the fusee, rotating it in a clockwise direction so the ratchet wheel on the underside of the fusee engages correctly with the two clicks on the steel ratchet wheel. Finally, fit the locking washer: align the holes in the locking washer with those in the arbor and, when you are happy that the two are aligned, take a length of tapered brass wire small enough in diameter for the front to fit easily through both the locking washer and fusee arbor. Push the wire through until it becomes tight. Test that when holding the edge of the great wheel, the fusee rotates anticlockwise smoothly and without too much friction. Also, test that the maintaining-power spring is working by rotating the fusee clockwise and letting go; it should return to the neutral position. Cut off the excess brass wire and smooth over the ends with pliers.

45 Pinning up the fusee.

## The Fusee Chain

If the chain is in good condition and both the hooks are good, then it only needs a light oiling. If the chain is stiff and discoloured, it needs

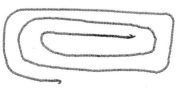

46 Fusee chain.

a little more attention. Take a length of peg wood about 5mm in diameter and 20cm long, cut a slot in one end, hold the peg wood upright in a vice with the chain held across the slot and place a few drops of oil on the chain, then pull it backwards and forwards through the slot, moving up and down the entire length of the chain. Do this until the chain feels reasonably free. Wipe the excess oil from the chain with a paper towel.

If, however, the chain is broken (a very common cause of a fusee watch not running), then it needs to be either replaced or repaired (*see* 'Repairing a Broken Fusee Chain').

When choosing a replacement chain, it is important that this is of a similar length and also the same thickness as the original chain. If the replacement chain is thicker than the original one, it may not fit the groove cut into the fusee, and if it is too thin, there is the possibility that it will not be strong enough for the spring and subsequently break owing to the strain on it. If the original chain is missing, then you can check whether a replacement one is the correct length by fixing the hook at the start of the fusee and winding it on to the groove until you reach the top (just below the spur). There should be a minimum 3cm of the chain left to attach onto the barrel. A little longer is not problematic, but any shorter will probably lead to the chain breaking when the watch is first wound up, owing to the stop iron not engaging in time. Too long a chain will also cause problems as the extra length of chain may catch the next section as it winds onto the barrel.

When fitting a chain it is important to fit the end with the plain hook on to the fusee and the end with the pointed hook on to the barrel. The reason is that the pointed hook is designed to act as a safety device. If for any reason during winding the fusee stop fails, so you continue to wind the fusee chain off the barrel, the point on the hook should push the hook out of the slot on the barrel. This is not ideal as it will release all the energy stored in the mainspring in one go, but it is better than breaking the fusee chain.

## Repairing a Broken Fusee Chain

If the fusee chain is broken but both parts are present (and both hooks are in good condition), it is possible to join them back together. A fusee chain consists of a number of steel links riveted together with steel pins, much like a miniature version of a modern bicycle chain.

Take one piece of the broken chain and, using a craft knife, carefully lever away any damaged links. When you have finished it should either have two outer parts or one central piece as illustrated. Prepare the other piece of the chain so it has the opposite arrangement to the first piece of chain.

Make sure that all pieces of the original rivet have been removed from both ends by pushing them through with the end of a broach or other sharp point. The old pin may need to be brought level with the link's surface, using an Arkansas stone, before it can be pushed out owing to the ends of the rivet being slightly flared. This operation is tricky and will take a great deal of patience.

Take a small diameter piece of soft steel wire (steel pins designed to pin clock plates together are ideal) and sharpen the end on a stone so it is tapered and can fit through the holes in both parts of the fusee chain.

Hold both pieces of the chain together so the holes line up, and push the pin through all three parts. Check that both hooks are on the same side of the chain.

47 Parts of a fusee chain prior to being joined.

**48** Fitting a new rivet to repair a broken fusee chain.

Place the assembly over a suitably sized hole on the staking tool and, using a flat-faced punch, lightly tap the pin so that it is a tight fit. Cut off the excess on both sides, as close to the chain as possible. Then, using an Arkansas stone, remove most of the pin, leaving only a small amount (approximately 0.25mm on either side). Place the chain on a flat, hard steel surface and tap the top of the pin until it is flattened into the link, then turn over and repeat on the other side. Smooth off flush with an Arkansas stone. Run it through your fingers to check for any roughness. Pull the chain to check its strength.

The above process can also be used on lengths of scrap fusee chains, so never throw these away. Always make sure that both pieces of chain are of the same size.

Sometimes, due to damage, the two pieces of chain are not long enough, in which case you will need to let in a new section of fusee chain; join all three lengths as described above.

# The Mainspring

Somewhere around the early 1400s, the mainspring was introduced as an alternative means of providing motive power to a clock. Prior to this, all clocks had been weight-driven. The introduction of the mainspring allowed a more compact design and, for the first time, the possibility of a 'portable' clock became a reality. This did not mean the end of weight-driven clocks, as there were a number of technical problems with springs, the major one being uneven power transfer to the train as the mainspring runs down, which in turn leads to variations in the rate of the clock. Other problems include increased maintenance and manufacturing costs. Early spring-driven clocks also needed to be wound quite often, every ten to twelve hours. The use of the coiled mainspring led ultimately to the first pocket watch made in the very early part of the sixteenth century.

The mainspring, as used in a pocket watch, consists of a length of spring steel wound into a spiral and fitted inside a brass case – the barrel. The inner end of the spring has a punched hole,

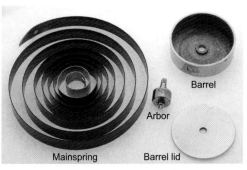

49 Dismantled mainspring barrel showing mainspring, arbor and barrel.

which engages with a hook on the barrel arbor. The outer end of the spring is fixed inside of the barrel either via a riveted hook on the end of the mainspring, which fits into a hole in the barrel, or via a hole at the end of the mainspring, which then fits over a hook on the inside of the barrel.

## Removing the Mainspring

Using a screwdriver fitted into the large slot on the top of the barrel, lever the top of the barrel up and remove it. Using pliers, twist the mainspring arbor anticlockwise to free it from the end of the mainspring and lift it clear. Place the end of a screwdriver under the inner end of the mainspring and turn the

barrel over so that the open end of the barrel is pointing away from you. Slowly rotate the screwdriver so it unwinds the mainspring, making sure you keep hold of the mainspring and barrel so that they do not fly off. Be careful, as the end of the mainspring can sometimes be sharp.

50 Assembled mainspring barrel.

## Refitting the Mainspring

In an ideal world you should use a mainspring winder, a tool specially designed for the job of fitting a mainspring into the barrel, but if you do not have access to one of these, then the following method can be used. First, fit the outer end of the mainspring: depending on the type of fixing, either fit the hole in the end of the mainspring over the hook on the inside of the barrel or fit the hook on the end of the mainspring into the hole in the barrel. While holding the end of the mainspring in place, feed the mainspring into the barrel while rotating the barrel. Keep doing this until the mainspring is fully into the barrel. Fit the

51 Barrel and mainspring showing riveted hook on mainspring.

barrel arbor and make sure that the hook on the arbor engages correctly with the hole at the inner end of the mainspring. If the end of the mainspring is too loose around the arbor, then use pliers to close the end a little. Apply a small amount of oil to the mainspring and then fit the cover, which is a 'snap' fit and so you may need to apply pressure by pressing down on a block of wood in order to get it to snap back into position.

## Problems that Occur with Mainsprings

- Broken mainspring.
- Damage to inner or outer fixing hole on mainspring.
- Loose barrel cover.
- Distorted or damaged barrel.
- Damaged fusee hook mounting point.
- Mainspring binding inside barrel.

### Replacing a Broken Mainspring

A broken mainspring is probably the single most common cause of a watch not working. Because there is a large amount of energy stored in a fully wound mainspring, when it breaks, it can also cause other problems, such as a broken fusee chain.

Although I have seen examples of a broken mainspring being riveted together, this is not to be recommended; the best solution is to replace it. You need to choose a replacement mainspring that has a similar length and the same height as the original mainspring, also choose one with a similar strength. If you fit a mainspring that is a lot weaker than the original one, the watch may struggle to run, as there will be insufficient energy to drive the train. Conversely, if you fit a mainspring that is much stronger that the original one, this may cause damage to the watch; particularly at risk is the fusee chain.

Fit the replacement mainspring into the barrel and check that it is of the correct length. The mainspring should occupy approximately one-third of the radius of the barrel. If it is too large, you need to remove it from the barrel and break off a short length from the outer end, then check again that it is the correct length. Once you are satisfied that the mainspring is the correct length, if not already present, you will need to punch a hole in the outer end. Heat approximately 1cm of the very end of the spring until it is red hot, and then allow it to cool by removing it slowly from the flame. Place the end on a staking tool over a hole about 3mm in diameter and then, using a punch with a sharp pointed end, drive the punch into the spring using a hammer.

52 Forming a new mounting hole at the outer end of a mainspring.

53 Opening up a newly formed hole on the outer end of a mainspring.

This should produce a small hole with a conical projection.

File off the projection and then using a cutting broach, open up the hole until it is big enough to fit over the hook on the inside of the barrel.

### Damaged Inner or Outer Fixing Hole on Mainspring

A damaged outer end fixing hole can be repaired as detailed above for replacing a broken mainspring. The inner end of the mainspring can be a little more difficult. Break off the damaged section of the mainspring; then, using pliers, pull out the centre section of the mainspring and heat it until it is red hot (be careful not to heat any other part of the mainspring). Allow it to cool slowly and then put the inner end on a staking tool and punch a hole, as detailed above, then open the hole out with a cutting broach. Using pliers, form the inner end of the mainspring so that it is the same diameter as the mainspring arbor and wrap right round it.

### Loose Barrel Cover

The barrel cover should 'snap' into place in the groove cut round the top of the barrel. If the barrel cover is a little loose, and therefore prone to pop off, you need to increase the overall diameter of the cover: place it on the table of a staking tool, with

54 Fixing a loose barrel lid.

the inner surface uppermost. Then, using a flat-faced punch, lightly tap the edge of the barrel cover while turning it until you have done this all the way around. Try the barrel cover to see if it now snaps into place; if not, try repeating the above process until it does.

## Distorted or Damaged Barrel

If the bottom of the barrel has become distorted, it might be possible to rectify the problem by placing the barrel, open end uppermost, on the table of a staking tool and, using a flat-faced punch, lightly tap over the inner surface until the bottom is made flat.

55 Fixing a distorted or damaged barrel.

## Loose Barrel Arbor

Hold the top and bottom of the barrel arbor between your thumb and forefinger, then try and move the barrel up and down by the edge; there should be very little movement of the barrel. If, however, the barrel is loose, you will need to re-bush the pivot holes. Dismantle the barrel as detailed in 'Removing the Mainspring'.

Take a length of brass tube whose internal diameter is very slightly less than the diameter of the barrel arbor pivot (note the top and bottom pivots are usually different sizes) and cut off a section that is the same depth as the hole to be re-bushed. Using a cutting broach, and working from the inside, open the original pivot hole until the new bush is a tight fit. Place the barrel or barrel lid (depending on which one is being re-bushed) on a staking tool and, using a flat-faced punch, tap the new bush into the hole until the bush is flush with the inside of the barrel. Check to see if the arbor pivot fits the newly bushed hole and adjust as necessary, using a cutting broach. Repeat if necessary for the other arbor pivot.

### Damaged Fusee Hook Mounting Point

If the fusee hook mounting hole has become damaged so that the fusee hook can no longer remain con-nected, you will need to form a new hole. Mark the position of the new hole with a punch and then using a 0.5mm drill form

56 Using a cutting broach to increase the size of the fusee hook mounting.

the new hole at a tangent to the barrel. Once the hole has been drilled, check that the fusee hook can engage with it correctly, if it is too small; open the hole up with a cutting broach.

# Hands

The hands that are fitted to a pocket watch play a very important part in the overall look of the watch, so you need to pay a great deal of attention to fitting the correct ones. If you are not sure which style of hands would best suit your watch, then either visit museum collections or consult reference books to get an idea of the most appropriate hands.

Most watches are fitted with either gold or blued steel hands. There can be quite a lot of variation in colour, particularly with gold hands, so it is important to make sure that the hour and minute hands match.

The hour hand is a friction fit over the hour wheel pipe. The minute hand is also a friction fit over the square end of the cannon pinion, the sides of which are very slightly tapered.

## Choosing the Correct Hands

The hour hand needs to be long enough for the tip of the hand to fall between the bottom edge of the numeral and approximately one-quarter of the way up the numeral. The minute hand needs to be chosen so that the point comes to the outer edge of the minute divisions on the chapter ring. The end of the second hand needs to come to the edge of the seconds' divisions on a flat dial and just short of them on a dial with a sunken seconds dial.

## Replacement Hands

If you are lucky, you will be able to reuse the existing hands, but quite often these will either be missing or damaged and, therefore, you will need to fit replacement ones. As with most watch parts, it is worth keeping an eye out for watch hands and purchasing them for spares, especially replacement second hands, which may prove to be difficult to obtain.

A replacement hour hand must have the same-sized hole as the outer diameter of the hour wheel pipe. If an hour hand cannot be found with the same-sized hole, then it is sometimes possible to change the size of the hole slightly. To increase the size of the hole, place the hand on the staking tool, over a hole just slightly larger than that of the hand, then place a long, tapered punch through the hole on the hand and tap the punch lightly. Be careful not to use too much force or you might split the ring. To make the hole smaller, place the hand on a staking tool (on an area without any holes) with the front facing down. Place a staking tool with a cone slightly larger than the rear tube, over the hand and lightly tap it. The effect should be to close the tube enough to make a tight fit on the hour wheel. If you close the tube too much, open it out again by using the method for enlarging the hole, as detailed above.

57 Closing the tube on an hour hand.

The minute hand is slightly more complex in that there are two methods used to fix them. On almost all full plate movements, the minute hand has a square cut into it; this is a friction fit over the end of the cannon pinion. The replacement needs to be close in size to the original. With gold hands, if the square is too large, it can be made smaller by placing it face down on a staking tool and, using a flat-faced punch, tapping it a few times. This has the effect of spreading the metal and, therefore, making the square hole a little smaller. If the square hole in the hand is smaller than the cannon pinion square, then it can be made larger by filing it; hold the hand in a pin vice and use a needle file with a square profile. It is very important to be careful that you hold the end of the hand near the hole and not by the hand itself.

The other fitting style for the minute hand (used almost always on half and three-quarter plate movements) has a round hole and is held in place by a friction fit on the end of the cannon pinion. If the hands are gold, the hole can be closed in the same way as a hand with a square fitting. If it is too small, the hole can be opened with a cutting broach.

These techniques can be tried with steel hands, but owing to the hardness of the steel, it may be difficult to carry them out successfully.

The second hand is held in place by a tube fitted over the extended pivot from the fourth wheel. To fit a new one, you may need to open the tube with a cutting broach in order to get it to fit.

# Internal Parts of a Watch

## The Balance Spring

Robert Hooke (1635–1703) was a true polymath, investigating a wide range of scientific phenomena, and was probably the first person to propose the use of a spring to control the rate of oscillation of the balance around 1657–58 – his idea being to use a straight spring. There is no evidence that he ever tried out his idea. Both Christiaan Huygens (1629–95) and Jean d'Hautefeuille are credited with actually fitting a balance spring to a watch or clock; Thomas Tompion (1638–1713) may have also done so independently. Christiaan Huygens is documented as applying a spiral spring to a balance in 1675. Whoever may have been responsible, the result was a step change in the ability of watches to measure time accurately (better than ten minutes in twenty-four hours) and, therefore, for the first time a watch became something more than an interesting piece of jewellery.

All the work on balance springs was carried out on the verge escapement and so by the time the lever escapement came into being, the balance spring was well established as a means of controlling the oscillations of the balance.

The balance spring's job is to return the balance to its neutral position after the impulse jewel is given a push by the action of the lever. Without the balance spring, the balance would swing until the impulse jewel hit the outer edge of the lever. In fact, unlike the verge escapement, the lever escapement could not function without a balance spring.

The balance assembly, if left undisturbed, would normally sit with the impulse jewel engaged with the lever fork and the lever central between the banking pins. If the balance is given a nudge, it will oscillate about this neutral position until all the energy imparted to it has dissipated. The rate at which the balance swings is known as its period of oscillation and is a constant for any balance and balance spring combination. It is this period of oscillation that determines the rate at which a watch runs. The three main things that affect the rate of oscillation of a balance are the mass of the balance, the 'springiness' of the balance spring and its length. It is this last factor that is used to regulate the rate of a watch (*see* the section 'The Regulator or Index').

The balance spring consists of a piece of sprung steel, usual blued, wound into a tight coil and fixed at the inner end to a brass collet on the balance. The outer end is fixed to the balance spring stud on the top plate or balance cock by means of a small, tapered brass pin.

## Lever Safety Action

In its normal state, the lever is held in place against the banking pins by draw because the angle of the escape wheel teeth relative to those of the lever pallets creates a small force. This holds the lever in place. As the balance swings backwards and forwards, the impulse jewel enters the fork at the end of the lever and, owing to the inertia of the balance, overcomes the draw and releases the next escape wheel tooth. The lever is then flipped over by the escape wheel, imparting energy to the balance and keeping it swinging.

If a watch were to receive a jolt, perhaps owing to being

carried in the pocket, it is possible that the knock could overcome the draw and the lever could flip over and, therefore, be
on the wrong side to receive the impulse jewel. The balance
will stop swinging and the watch will stop.

To prevent this from happening, a safety pin is fitted to
the end of the lever. This pin is positioned so that it 'passes'
the crescent cut into the edge of the table roller. If the watch
receives a jolt, which causes the lever to move, the safety pin will
connect with the
edge of the table
roller and prevent
the lever from
getting out of syn-
chronization with
the impulse jewel.

58 Lever showing safety pin.

## Escape Wheel

The escape wheel used in a typical
post-1820s English fusee lever is
known as a ratchet tooth escape
wheel and almost always has fifteen
teeth; the pinion will usually have
seven leaves.

59 Ratchet-toothed escape wheel.

## Wheels and Pinions

In a typical English fusee lever there are four wheels (great,
centre, third and fourth). The great wheel is part of the fusee.

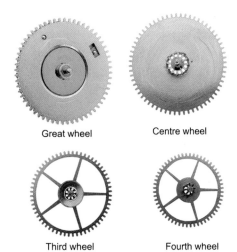

Great wheel       Centre wheel

Third wheel       Fourth wheel

The centre, third and fourth wheels are each fitted to an arbor, the ends of which are formed into pivots; the arbor also carries the pinion.

60 Great, centre, third and fourth wheels.

## Motion Work and Cannon Pinion

61 Cannon pinion.

For a watch to be practically useful there needs to be a way of indicating the time to the owner. In a pocket watch this is usually done by fitting hands, which indicate the hours, minutes and seconds on the dial. For the hands to be able to do this, they need to be connected to the moving parts of the watch. This is achieved via the cannon pinion and motion work.

The cannon pinion consists of a steel tube with teeth around the base, the top is shaped to allow the minute hand to be fitted, square for front-set hands (usually full plate movements), round for rear-set hands (half and three-quarter plate movements). The cannon pinion is fitted over the centre wheel arbor and is a 'friction' fit on the arbor. In normal use there is sufficient friction between the centre wheel arbor and cannon pinion for both to rotate together. However, when the hands need to be set, the cannon pinion will 'slip' on the centre wheel arbor to allow this to happen.

The cannon pinion carries the minute hand and makes one complete rotation every hour. The hour wheel is a loose fit over the cannon pinion and is connected to it via the minute wheel. The minute and hour wheels convert the hourly rotation of the cannon pinion into the twelve-hourly rotation required by the hour hand.

62 Hour and minute wheels.

## Watch Glasses (Crystals)

Most watches will have a clear glass cover over the dial and hands to protect them from dirt and damage. The glass cover, also known as a crystal, is manufactured in a wide range of sizes and thicknesses. They also come in a wide variety of shapes from completely flat to high dome and bull's eye.

The watch glass is fitted into a small groove around the top of the bezel and, in an ideal world, is of a size so that it can be 'popped' into position and stay in place without the use of glue. If you intend to take up watch repairing as a hobby, it will be useful to build up a stock of old watch glasses covering the most popular sizes.

63 Three examples of watch glasses.

If the watch still has its original watch glass, it is best not to try and remove it unless it is badly scratched, as it is possible that it may become damaged around the edge. If it is badly damaged or missing, you will need to replace it. This can be either with a plastic one (not great) or, much better, by a glass one. The latter can still be brought from auctions (usually only as a number of watch glasses sold as a lot). There are also some people who will sell just one specific watch glass, if you supply the required diameter. As stated above, the watch glass should be chosen so that it 'pops' into place and does not require any glue to hold it in place. In practice, you will not always have the exact size and, therefore, it may need to be glued in place. Use soft glue that can easily be removed later, if necessary. Once it has dried, remove any excess glue with a piece of peg wood, sharpened to a point, so as not to damage the case.

When choosing a suitable watch glass make sure that it is not only the correct diameter but also that it is high enough to accommodate the hands and cannon pinion. There should be sufficient space to allow the hands to move freely. As you close the front bezel, make sure that the end of the minute hand is not pressed down, as this can cause it to catch on the hour hand and stop the watch.

## Screws

On English high-quality watches it is common to find screws marked with punched dots, which correspond with dots marked next to the screw position. The reason for this was that most screws on English watches were handmade and, therefore, it was important to make sure that they were fitted in the correct location.

*Tightening Screws*

It is very important that you do not over-tighten any screw. When tightening a screw, stop as soon as you feel resistance. If you apply more force after this point, you run the risk of damaging the screw, the threaded hole into which the screw is fitted or your screwdriver; you will also annoy any future watchmaker who has to work on the watch.

## The Regulator or Index

For any given balance, the effective length of the balance spring governs the rate of oscillation; this in turn determines the rate at which the watch runs. The device that controls the length of the balance spring is known as the regulator or index.

Early English lever pocket watches used the Bosley-type of regulator, as used in English verges of the time. This was joined by the London quadrant and a variation where the regulator lever is moved across a scale on the back of the balance cock.

In its simplest form, the regulator consists of a simple arm that extends from a sprung ring that passes through a hole in the top plate, and which holds the index pins (sometimes referred to as curb pins). The regulator arm can move backwards and forwards across a scale marked on the top plate. The movement of the regulator arm also moves the index pins and, thereby, lengthens (slows the rate of the balance) or shortens (quickens the rate of the balance) the effective length of the balance spring.

64 Full plate movement with Bosley-type regulator.

65 Full plate movement with London quadrant regulator.

66 Three-quarter plate movement with regulator on balance cock.

# Dismantling a Watch

## Removing the Hands

Before you can remove the hands, you will need to open the front bezel by inserting a case knife under the lug between 1 and 2 o'clock on an open-faced watch and lever up the bezel. If the watch is a full or half hunter, first open the outer cover and then insert a case knife under the lug at 6 o'clock and lever up the bezel.

67 Opening the front bezel using a case knife.

The second hand can be removed by using a thin-bladed lever placed under the second hand where it is connected to its pivot and then levering it up, keeping a finger over the second hand to stop it flying off. Place a small piece of paper under the lever to prevent damage to the dial. The hour and minute hands

68 Removing the hands using a tool especially designed for the job.

are best removed using a hand-removing tool. Press the plunger down and place the tool over the hands, release the plunger and allow the two claws to fit under the hour hand. Press down on the handle and the claws should lever up the hands.

## Removing the Movement from the Case

69 Removing a full plate movement from a double-bottomed case.

To remove a movement from a double-bottomed case, open the front bezel and push out the pin at 12 o'clock using a piece of blued steel just smaller in diameter then the case pin; sometimes you might need to give the end a light tap to free the pin. The retaining pin is usually slightly tapered and, by convention, should have been inserted from the right-hand side, so pressure should be applied from the left-hand side. Just be aware that the pin may have been inserted from the left. Sometimes the pin will have become stuck, maybe due to it being steel and having become rusted in place. If this happens, try dripping a small amount of oil on the hinge and leaving for twenty-four hours before repeating the above process.

## Removing the Dust Cap

70 Dust cap showing retaining clip.

- For a standard dust cap, using your nail, push the small pip (mid-way along the retaining clip) clockwise until it stops. Lift the dust cap vertically and place aside.

- For a rim dust cap, turn the two retaining screws until the modified heads are clear of the edge of the dust cap. Carefully lever up the dust cap and place aside.

71 Shaped screws used to hold a rim dust cap in place.

- For a spring-up dust cap (most often, but not exclusively, found on half and three-quarter plate move-

72 Removing the retaining pin from a spring-load dust cap.

ments), using your nail, press the small lever at the edge of the bottom plate. The dust cap should flip up. If the spring is damaged, you may need to manually lift the dust cap.

## Removing the Dial

The dial is nearly always held in place by brass tapered pins; the dial foot passes through a hole in the bottom plate and is fixed in place by a tapered brass pin that fits through a hole at the end of the dial foot. Some watches use an intermediate plate

73 Bottom plate showing dial retaining pin.

between the bottom plate and the dial known as a dial plate. When the dial is fitted via a dial plate, the dial feet are much shorter but are still fixed to the dial plate using tapered brass pins; the dial and dial plate are then pinned to the bottom plate. The dial plate usually also carries the movement hinge.

To remove a dial, carefully pull each tapered brass pin out with a pair of tweezers. Sometimes a pin may be too tightly fitted to allow its removal with tweezers, in which case try to grip the end of the pin with cutters (only use very light pressure as you do not want to cut through the pin) and carefully lever back the cutters against the edge of the top plate of the move-

74 Underside of a dial showing dial plate.

ment (protect the edge of the movement with a small piece of paper). Once all the pins have been removed, carefully lift the dial clear of the bottom plate. Try to keep the dial perpendicular to the bottom plate as you remove it, as this avoids the risk that you might strain the dial feet and damage the front of the dial. If the dial is mounted via a dial plate, having removed the dial and dial plate, you need to remove the pins that hold the dial to the dial plate using tweezers.

On some very high-quality watches you might find that the dial is held in place by screws in the edge of the bottom plate. To remove the dial, slacken all three screws and lever up the

75 Full plate movement with dial removed showing motion work.

dial; care should be taken to make sure that all three screws are fully disengaged from the dial feet before trying to remove the dial.

Once the dial has been removed, lift the motion work and, if fitted, the dial washer away, and place them in the storage tray.

Remove the cannon pinion by fitting a pin vice over the cannon pinion and tightening the pin vice, then, with a twisting action, pull the pin vice upwards. Be careful not to apply any sideways force, as this may bend or break the centre wheel arbor on which the cannon pinion is fitted.

76 Removing the cannon pinion from a full plate movement.

## Removing the Balance

For full plate movements the balance is always mounted on the top plate. This leads to a movement that is easier to make and service but is quite thick. The issue of thickness is addressed in both the half and three-quarter plate movement's layout, as the design allows the overall thickness to be reduced.

77 Half plate movement made by Richard Hornly.

This is achieved by mounting the balance on the bottom plate.

With the movement placed in a movement holder, unscrew the balance cock retaining screw and carefully lift up the balance cock with tweezers and place in the storage tray. Always

78 Three-quarter plate movement
by Benjamin Gaunt, Barnsley.

remember that, especially with
the London quadrant regulator,
there is a risk that, as you lift the
balance up, the index pins can
catch on the balance spring and
damage or distort it. Another
issue is that the oil used on the
pivot may have become sticky
with age and, therefore, holds on
to the top pivot of the balance as
you lift the balance cock away.

## For Movements with a London Quadrant Regulator

Unscrew the arm that carries the
balance spring and carefully lift
the balance assembly clear of the
top plate.

79 Full plate movement with London
quadrant regulator, balance cock removed.

## For Movements with a Bosley-Type Regulator

80 Full plate movement with Bosley
regulator, balance cock removed.

Using tweezers, push the brass
pin out of the balance spring
stud. Carefully feed the balance
spring clear of the stud and lift
the balance assembly away from
the top plate.

## For Half and Three-Quarter Plate Movements

Unscrew the balance cock retaining screw and remove the screw. Carefully lever the balance cock up until it is free of the bottom plate and lift it clear. Depending on the design, the balance assembly will come away with the balance cock (balance spring attached to balance cock) or remain in place (balance spring attached to an

81 Half plate movement, balance cock removed.

arm screwed to the top plate). In the latter case, you need to unscrew the retaining arm and lift the balance assembly away from the movement.

These are the most common types of movement but there are other variations for fixing the balance spring, particularly with half and three-quarter plate movements. In all cases, pay particular care as to where the balance spring is attached before removing the balance cock.

82 Removing the balance cock from a three -quarter plate movement.

## Letting Down the Mainspring

Before any further work in dismantling the movement can be carried out, it is vitally important that the mainspring is let down (removing all tension in the mainspring); failure to do so could lead to severe damage to the movement and to the repairer!

In theory, the ideal way to let down the mainspring is to use a key fitted over the end of the mainspring arbor, where it protrudes above the setup ratchet (there needs to be at least 2mm of the arbor above the ratchet). Slacken the screw that holds the ratchet pawl, turn the key slightly clockwise so that it takes the tension off the ratchet and allows the ratchet pawl to be disengaged. Push the pawl away from the ratchet and, while keeping a firm grip on the key, allow it to slowly turn between your thumb and figures until all the tension has been released.

However, in my experience, I have not found the above method to be reliable, as the arbor is usually too short to safely fit the key over it. For this reason I would advise the following way to let down the mainspring. Fit a pin vice to the winding arbor and tighten it, then place the pin vice in a bench vice.

83 Winder held by pin vice while letting down the mainspring.

84 Removing the fusee chain.

While holding the movement so that it cannot rotate, unscrew the two retaining screws on the third-wheel bridge and carefully lift the bridge clear, while maintaining your hold on the movement. Lift up the third wheel and remove it from the movement. Replace the bridge and screw in place. Allow the movement to slowly turn, while keeping a firm hold on it, as there is a lot of energy stored in the mainspring. Continue until all the tension in the mainspring has been released.

Remove the pin vice and then, holding the movement with the bottom plate uppermost, remove the third-wheel bridge and loosen the ratchet pawl retaining screw and release the remaining tension in the mainspring by pushing the pawl clear of the ratchet. Remove the ratchet wheel. Pull the fusee chain away from the movement (the barrel should rotate as the chain unwinds) so that the hook on the barrel can be released. Then

rotate the fusee so the other end of the fusee chain can be unhooked.

Unscrew the two screws that hold the barrel bridge in place. Lift the barrel bridge clear and place it in the storage tray with its screws. Lift the barrel clear and also place it in the storage tray.

85 Movement with balance, barrel and barrel bridge removed.

## Removing the Top Plate (Full Plate Movement)

The top plate is held in place by four tapered brass pins. To remove these use a pair of strong tweezers placed as shown in the illustration and push together. If all goes well, the pin should pop out. Sometimes the pin may be too firmly pushed home and you might need

86 Using tweezers to push out one of the brass pins holding the top plate in place.

to use pliers to overcome the tight fit; be careful not to mark the top plate. It is usual for two of the pins to be short, only

87 Using a piece of blued steel, whose end has been sharpened, to push out a short pin.

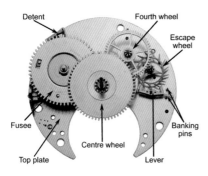

88 Underside view of the top plate with fusee, fourth wheel, escape wheel and lever.

Detent   Fourth wheel   Escape wheel   Banking pins   Lever   Centre wheel   Top plate   Fusee

89 Underside view of top plate with all parts removed showing fusee stop.

just protruding either side of the pillar. They are the one under the barrel bridge and the one under the balance cock. Because these pins are short, the above method may not work; instead you may need to push them out using a length of blued steel with the end sharpened to a point.

Once all the pins have been removed, you can lift the top plate clear of the pillars on the bottom plate. While lifting the top plate clear, pay particular attention to the lever, because it fits between the top plate and balance potance; it must remain with the top plate, otherwise you might bend or break the lever pivots. The other part to keep an eye on is the fusee maintaining-power detent as this can spring off.

Once separated, carefully lift the lever clear from the top plate and place it in the storage tray. Proceed to remove the fusee maintaining-power detent, fusee, escape, fourth and centre wheels. It is important when removing wheels that you only lift them straight up to avoid damaging their pivots or pivot holes. Place all the parts in the storage tray. Remove the screw that holds the potance in place and lift the potance clear.

Unscrew the fusee stop iron spring retaining screw and remove the spring. Push out the brass pin that holds the fusee stop iron in place and remove the fusee stop iron. If the watch has a Bosley-type regulator, remove this by pushing a piece of peg wood under the regulator arm and lever it away from the top plate.

90 Bottom plate with catch removed.

Dismantle the main-spring (*see* the section 'Removing the Mainspring') and fusee (*see* the section 'Fusee Repairs'). Unscrew and remove the mainspring setup ratchet pawl and fusee maintaining-power detent spring. To remove the case catch, unscrew the retaining screw (make sure you hold the catch while doing this as otherwise it could fly off). Unscrew and remove the catch spring.

If fitted, remove the start/stop mechanism. This then completes the dismantling of the bottom plate.

91 Stop/start mechanism.

# Dismantling a Half or Three-Quarter Plate Movement

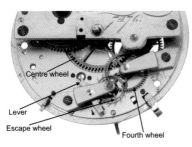

92 Half plate movement with balance removed.

93 Half plate movement with escape wheel and lever removed.

94 Half plate movement with fourth wheel removed.

Having let down the mainspring, unscrew the retaining screw on the escape wheel cock and carefully lift the cock straight up. Lift up the lever and escape wheel and place all the items in the storage tray.

For half plate movements there is an additional cock for the fourth wheel. Unscrew the retaining screw and lift the fourth wheel cock vertically to avoid the risk of bending or breaking the pivot (note the bottom pivot protrudes beyond the bottom plate to form the second-hand arbor).

Before the top plate can be removed, you need to remove the hand setting arbor. This is a friction fit through the centre wheel. Place the movement on a stacking tool bottom plate uppermost; the hand setting square should be over a small 'cup' (place paper towel or masking tape over the cup to prevent damage to the surface of the top plate). Using a flat-faced punch, tap the hand setting arbor lightly until it is pushed out and place in storage tray.

Some half and three-quarter plate movements have a bridge holding the barrel in place. If so, remove the two retaining screws and lift the bridge clear. Lift the barrel clear of the movement.

95 Half plate movement on staking tool, removing the hand setting arbor.

Most half and three-quarter plate movement use three screws to fix the top plate to the bottom plate. Remove all three screws and carefully lift the top plate straight up, again being careful not to damage any pivots. Once the top plate is clear, remove the barrel (if still present), detent, fusee, third, fourth (if a three-quarter plate movement) and centre wheels. Remove all the remaining parts, such as the catch, fusee stop iron and detent spring.

## Centre Seconds Chronograph Movements

The centre seconds chronograph pocket watch has a three-quarter plate movement and started to appear in the 1870s; it remained popular until the 1900s. Usually it was quite a large, open-faced watch with a slide stop button at 2 o'clock. The dial is almost always marked 'CENTRE SECONDS CHRONOGRAPH' and the outer chapter ring is marked in one-fifth of a second (0 to 300). The stop button moves a small

96 Centre seconds chronograph.

lever on the edge of the movement and this in turn moves a shaped piece of wire that comes into contact with the edge of the table roller and, thereby, stops the whole movement.

Centre seconds chronographs are sometime referred to as doctors' watches, I assume because they have a large second hand. I have found no evidence that this, or come to that, any other pocket watch was designed specifically for use by a doctor. Any watch with a second hand can be used to take the pulse of a patient.

This sort of watch should not be confused with one described as a chronometer, a type of watch, usually with a detent escapement, that was designed to be very accurate and mainly used for the measurement of longitude at sea.

The term chronograph is now more usually associated with a design of watch that has an independent centre seconds hand, which can be started, stopped and returned to zero via a button, without affecting the normal running of the watch.

From the point of view of servicing and repairing centre seconds chronograph pocket watches, they should be dealt with in the same way as other three-quarter plate watches, apart from the way the movement is removed from the case.

The movement is held in place by a hinge at 12 o'clock and a pin at 6 o'clock, which protrudes from the edge of the move-ment and engages with a hole on the rim of the case. To remove the movement, open the front bezel, using a case knife, then push out the movement retaining pin at 12 o'clock. As with other watches, this pin is slightly tapered with the thinner end on the left. Therefore, to remove the retaining pin, you should push from the left side. Once the movement retaining pin has been removed, lift the movement up at the 12 o'clock position and pull the movement away in the direction of the pendant.

# Cleaning the Parts

Once the watch has been completely dismantled and all the parts placed in a storage tray, the next job is to clean each part. Most parts can be cleaned by soaking them in a suitable solvent, such as isopropanol alcohol, lighter fluid or paraffin (kerosene). Please be aware that most of the solvents used to clean watch parts are flammable and, therefore, great care should be used when handling them (always work in a well-ventilated area); some are also poisonous, so keep them locked away when not in use. Place the parts in a small bowl and cover with the solvent, then leave to soak for a few hours. It is not a good idea to place the lever or balance in the solvent as both these usually have jewelled parts, which will have been fixed in place with shellac, which dissolves in most solvents.

Remove each part from the solvent and carefully clean and dry it with a paper towel. Be very careful not to damage or distort the parts. The pinion leaves should be cleaned with a piece of peg wood cut to fit.

97 Cleaning between the leaves of a pinion using peg wood.

Any stubborn dirt can be removed with a small, stiff-bristled bush, dipped in the solvent. Screws can be cleaned by holding them firmly in a paper towel held between your thumb and finger and 'un-screwing' them with a screwdriver, which should remove any dirt from the threads. Repeat until clean.

The balance assembly is a little more difficult to clean. Be very careful not to damage the balance spring as it can easily become distorted by careless handling. Because the impulse jewel is usually held in place by shellac, the balance assembly should not be left in the cleaning solvent for any length of time. Place the balance assembly in the cleaning solvent (there are specific cleaners for balances) and gently agitate it for a minute or so. Remove the balance assembly from the solvent and carefully dry by blowing air over it using a hand-blower (as used to remove dust).

After cleaning, examine each part using a loupe and check for any damage. You are looking for missing teeth, bent pivots, distorted wheels and so on.

Once all the parts have been cleaned, the next job is to clean the pivot holes in the top plate, bottom plate and bridges. Take a piece of peg wood and sharpen the end to a point. Put the point in the pivot hole and rotate a few times. Remove the peg wood from the pivot hole and re-sharpen the end, repeat until the point comes out of the pivot hole clean. Do this from both sides of the pivot hole. Always use a freshly sharpened piece of peg wood to reduce the risk of it breaking off in the pivot hole. If the end of the peg wood does break off in a pivot hole, first

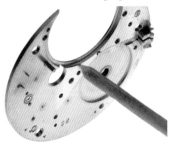

try pushing it out from the other side with a newly sharpened point on the peg wood. If this fails to push the obstructing piece of peg wood out, use a steel pin whose end has been brought to a very fine point on a sharpening stone. Use this with care, as it is very easy to damage the pivot hole.

98 Cleaning pivot holes with peg wood.

# Reassembling a Watch

## Full Plate Movement

D ab a small amount of oil on the end of the fusee stop iron where it connects to the top plate. Take the top plate and, holding it upside-down (inner surface uppermost), fit the fusee stop iron in place, then push the fixing pin through firmly. Check that the stop iron is free to move up and down; also check that the fixing pin does not interfere with any other parts, i.e. the bottom plate pillars. Fit the fusee stop iron spring so that the loose end goes under the fusee stop iron; there should be a slight hollow on the underside of the stop iron where the spring end should sit. Fit the retaining screw and tighten. The fusee stop iron should sit clear of the underside of the top plate and, when pushed down, should spring up again when released.

Fit the balance lower pivot potance, aligning the steady pins

99 Underside view of the top plate prior to assembly.

100 Top plate with fusee stop fitted.

101 Top plate with balance potance fitted.

102 Bottom plate showing maintaining-power detent spring.

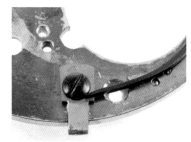

103 Bottom plate with catch fitted.

with the holes in the top plate. Fit the retaining screw and tighten. Put the top plate aside.

Take the bottom plate and, holding it with the pillars facing up (so you are looking at the inner surface), fit the detent spring and position it so that the free end is just over (towards the centre of) the hole that the detent fits into. Fit the retaining screw and tighten.

Turn the bottom plate over and fit the case catch and retaining screw; the screw should not be fully tightened but left loose enough for the catch to move backwards and forwards. Apply a small amount of oil around the head of the catch screw. Fit the catch spring and then its retaining screw and tighten. Using a piece of peg wood, push the free end of the catch spring towards the centre until it 'drops' behind the catch. Test the catch by pushing it and letting go; if all is well, it should move forwards under the action of the spring. Fit the setup ratchet pawl and screw. If the movement has a stop/start mechanism, fit this. Fit the maintaining-power detent so that it points to the left (*see* photo). Put the bottom plate aside.

104 Bottom plate showing position of detent prior to assembly.

Take the top plate and, using tweezers, first place the lever in its pivot hole, with the fork end under the balance potance. Next, place the escape wheel, fourth wheel, fusee and finally the centre wheel.

Keeping the top plate level, introduce the bottom plate with the pillar holes and pillars aligned. First allow the centre wheel arbor to enter its pivot hole, and then the lower pivot of the fusee (note the hole in the top plate is larger than the

105 Top plate with fusee, centre wheel, fourth wheel, escape wheel and lever fitted.

fusee pivot, the actual pivot hole is on the third-wheel bridge). By now the top of the pillars should start to engage with their respective holes in the top plate. While keeping both plates level, and maintaining light pressure across the plates, use tweezers to manipulate the pivots of the lever and escape wheel into their respective pivot holes (sometimes the lower pivot hole for the escape wheel is also on the third-wheel bridge). Next, manipulate the maintaining-power detent pivot into its pivot hole. Slowly push both plates together, making sure every part stays in place. Once the plates are full together, turn the assembly over (still keeping pressure on the plates) and fit the four brass pins, remembering to fit the two short ones in the correct locations (where the barrel bridge and balance cock are fitted).

Fit the third-wheel bridge and fix in place with both screws (do not fit the third wheel at this stage). Flip the maintaining-power detent over so that it engages with the maintaining-power ratchet. Using the correct-sized key, rotate the winding square a few times in both directions. If all is well with the fusee, it should rotate freely. In the clockwise direction, the centre

wheel should also rotate; in the anticlockwise direction, the upper part of the fusee should rotate but the great wheel should not move as the maintaining-power detent holds it. Fit the barrel and then the barrel bridge, fit the two retaining screws and tighten. Check that the barrel rotates freely.

106 Top and bottom plates pinned together with barrel and barrel bridge fitted.

## Half or Three-Quarter Plate Movement

Dab a small amount of oil on the end of the fusee stop iron where it connects to the top plate and fit in place, then push the fixing pin through firmly. Check that the stop iron is free to move up and down, also check that the fixing pin does not interfere with any other parts, i.e. the bottom plate pillars. Fit the fusee stop iron spring so that the loose end goes under

the fusee stop iron; there should be a slight hollow on the underside of the stop iron where the spring end should sit. Fit the retaining screw and tighten. The fusee stop iron should sit clear of

107 Half plate movement, top plate with fusee stop fitted.

the underside of the top plate and, when pushed down, should spring up again when released. Put the top plate aside.

Take the bottom plate and, holding it with the pillars facing up (so you are looking at the inner surface), fit the detent spring and position it so that the free end is just over (towards the centre of) the hole that the detent fits into. Fit the retaining screw and tighten.

Turn the bottom plate over and fit the case catch and retaining screw; the screw should not be fully tightened but left just loose enough for the catch to move backwards and forwards. Apply a small amount of oil around the head of the catch screw. Fit the catch spring and then its retaining screw and tighten. Using a piece of peg wood, push the free end of the catch spring towards the centre until it 'drops' behind the catch. Test the catch by pushing it in and letting go. If all is well, it should move forwards under the action of the spring.

108 Half plate movement, bottom plate with catch and setup ratchet pawl fitted.

If the dust cap is spring-loaded (common on half and three-quarter plate movements), fit its catch and spring in the same way as the case catch was fitted. If the movement has a stop/start mechanism, fit these

109 Half plate movement, bottom plate with start/stop work and dust cap spring-fitted.

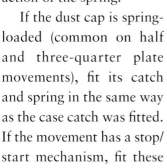

110 Half plate movement, bottom plate with fusee, detent, centre wheel and barrel fitted.

111 Half plate movement with top plate fitted.

parts too. Fit the setup ratchet pawl and screw.

Using tweezers, fit the centre wheel in place, and then fit the fusee in its pivot hole. Fit the maintaining-power detent so that it engages with the ratchet wheel on the fusee. The fusee detent should be held in place by the fusee detent spring. If the watch does not have a barrel bridge, now is the time to fit the barrel. If it is a three-quarter plate movement, fit the fourth wheel.

Keeping the bottom plate level, introduce the top plate, aligning the pillars with their corresponding mounting holes on the top plate. Allow the fusee winder to engage with its pivot hole and continue to lower the top plate; the top of the pillars should start to engage with their respective holes in the top plate. While keeping both plates level, and maintaining light pressure across the plates, use tweezers to manipulate the pivots of the centre and, if fitted, fourth wheel into their respective pivot holes. Then manipulate the maintaining-power detent pivot into its pivot hole. Slowly push both plates together, making sure every part stays in place. Once the plates are full together, fit the three retaining screws. While tightening the screws, make sure all parts are still in their correct positions.

Turn the movement over and fit the third wheel and third-wheel bridge, then fix in place with both screws. If you are assembling a half plate movement, turn it over and fit the fourth wheel and fourth wheel cock, then fit its retaining screw and tighten. Using the correct-sized key, rotate the winding square anti-clockwise; only the upper

112 Half plate movement, fitting third wheel and bridge.

part of the fusee should turn with the detent preventing the ratchet and the rest of the train from moving. Turn the winding square clockwise, the movement train should turn freely (be careful not to apply too much force to the key as it is possible to damage the train if run too fast).

If not already fitted, fit the barrel and then the barrel bridge, fit the two retaining screws and tighten. Check that the barrel rotates freely.

## Fitting the Fusee Chain

Fitting the fusee chain is quite a fiddly job, so take your time. Use a key to rotate the winding square until the fusee chain mounting point is brought to the outer edge of the movement. Holding the movement sideways with the barrel uppermost, feed the fusee chain, hook first (make sure it is the right

113 Hooking one end of the fusee chain onto the fusee.

114 Fusee chain after winding onto the barrel.

hook – the one without the small point), down between the barrel and movement pillars so that the hook comes out by the fusee. Using tweezers, fit the fusee chain hook onto the fusee and then, using a key, wind the fusee chain on to the fusee.

When most of the fusee chain has been wound on to the fusee, rotate the barrel until the hook slot is visible and fit the fusee chain barrel hook into the slot. While keeping a figure on the fusee chain to stop it coming loose, fit a suitably sized key over the barrel arbor, where it protrudes through the bottom plate, and slowly rotate the barrel in an anticlockwise direction, allowing the fusee chain to neatly wind onto the barrel from the fusee.

When all of the fusee chain has been wound onto the barrel, remove the key and fit the setup ratchet and engage the setup ratchet pawl. Using a piece of peg wood, push the setup ratchet wheel anticlockwise four to five teeth, while keeping light pressure on the setup ratchet pawl. This will put some tension on the fusee, even when the fusee chain has completely unwound from the fusee.

This is an approximation to the full process of setting up a fusee and mainspring, which would have originally been done using an adjusting rod and weights. The reason for not describing the full process is that when the watch movement was originally made, the groove cut into the fusee would have been calculated to match the mainspring. Over the life of the watch there is a very good chance that the mainspring will have broken and, therefore, been replaced and so the replacement mainspring is unlikely to have had the same characteristics as the original mainspring and, therefore, will not be a true match to the fusee. For this reason, it is not justifiable to go to the trouble of using an adjustment rod and weight.

## For Full Plate Movements

Once the mainspring has been set up, remove the third-wheel bridge and fit the third wheel, replace the third-wheel bridge and fixing screws. Fit the cannon pinion, place it over the centre wheel arbor and, using tweezers, press down until the cannon pinion reaches the bottom. Using a key, rotate the cannon pinion both clockwise and anti-clockwise; you should feel some resistance but the cannon pinion should also rotate smoothly.

115 Cannon pinion fitted to full plate movement.

## For Half and Three-Quarter Plate Movements

Place the lever and escape wheel in their respective pivot holes and fit the escape wheel cock. While keeping light pressure on the cock, use tweezers to manipulate the lever and escape wheel upper pivots into their respective pivot holes in the cock. Fit and tighten the retaining screw (as always, never fully

116 Half plate movement with fourth wheel, escape wheel and lever fitted.

117 Fitting hand setting arbor on a half plate movement.

118 Fitting the cannon to the hand setting arbor on a half plate movement.

tighten the retaining screw until you are sure all pivots are correctly positioned).

Fit the hand setting arbor by holding the movement with the top plate uppermost and push the hand setting arbor into the hole that runs through the centre wheel pinion. Place the movement on a staking tool and using a flat-faced punch, tap the hand setting arbor home.

Turn the movement over and fit the cannon pinion over the protruding end of the hand setting arbor; using a hollow punch, tap the cannon pinion home. Use a key to rotate the hand setting arbor both clockwise and anticlockwise; you should feel some resistance but the hand setting arbor should rotate smoothly.

## For All Movements

Apply a small amount of oil to each pivot top and bottom; do not forget to oil both balance pivots. To test that you have assembled the movement correctly, using a piece of peg wood, apply a small amount of pressure in a clockwise direction to the third wheel, if all is well, this should cause the lever to move backwards and forwards rapidly.

# Fitting the Balance Assembly

## London Quadrant Regulator

Using tweezers, carefully lift the balance assembly, holding it by the rim of the balance, and place the lower pivot into the balance potance. Rotate the balance until the arm that holds the balance spring is aligned with its mounting position and lower into place; there is a small pin on the underside of the arm that fits into a hole in the top plate.

119 Fitting balance on a full plate movement with London quadrant.

Once the arm is in place, fit the retaining screw, but before you tighten the retaining screw, make sure that the arm is correctly in position so that the balance spring is symmetrical. Using tweezers, adjust the position of the balance until the impulse jewel is positioned in between the lever fork. Put the balance cock in place so that its steady pins align with their corresponding holes in the top plate, being very careful not to press the balance cock onto the top plate at this stage, as it is very easy to bend or break the balance pivots. Holding the movement level, and looking in from the side, use tweezers to adjust the position of the top balance pivot until it engages

120 Index pins on a London quadrant regulator.

with its pivot hole in the balance cock. Check that the outer turn of the balance spring is between the regulator index pins. If not, carefully move the balance spring until it is between the index pins (you might need to slacken the screw that holds the arm and twist left or right to achieve this). Once you are happy that the balance pivots (top and bottom) are in their respective pivot holes, while keeping light pressure on the balance cock, give the movement a slight shake to check if the balance swings freely. If all is well, fit the balance cock retaining screw and carefully tighten it, all the time checking that the balance can still swing freely.

### Bosley Regulator

Using tweezers, carefully lift the balance assembly holding it by the rim of the balance, and place the lower pivot into the balance potance. Feed the end of the balance spring through the hole in the balance spring stud with tweezers. Continue to feed the balance spring through until the impulse jewel is

121 Fitting the balance on a full plate movement with Bosley regulator.

aligned between the lever fork horns. Fix the balance spring in place with a brass pin and lightly press home. Check that the outer turn of the balance spring is between the index pins on the regulator arm. Place the balance cock in place so that its steady pins align with their corresponding holes in the top plate, being very careful not to press the balance cock onto the top plate at this stage, as it is very easy to bend or break the balance pivots. Holding the movement level, and looking in from the side, use tweezers to adjust the position of the top balance pivot until it engages with its pivot hole in the balance cock. Once you are happy that the balance pivots (top and bottom) are in their respective pivot holes, while still keeping light pressure on the balance cock, give the movement a slight shake to check if the balance swings freely. If all is well, fit the balance cock retaining screw and carefully tighten it, all the time checking that the balance can still swing freely. Once the balance has stopped oscillating, check that the lever is mid-way between the banking pins. If the lever is not central between the banking pins, remove the balance cock and tapered brass pin and adjust the balance spring's position; feed more of the balance spring through the balance spring stud to move the lever to the right, pull the balance spring back to move the lever to the left. Replace the balance cock and check that the lever is now central between the banking pins and, if necessary, repeat the above until it is.

### Half and Three-Quarter Plate Movements – Balance Spring Fixed to an Arm

If the balance spring is held by an arm fixed to the top plate (the most common method), use tweezers to place the balance on the bottom plate with the lower pivot in its pivot hole. Position the arm on the edge of the top plate and

122 Fitting the balance on a half plate movement with balance spring held by an arm.

secure in place with the retaining screw. Move the balance so that the impulse jewel is engaged with the fork of the lever.

Lower the balance cock down on to the bottom plate so that the steady pins engage with their corresponding holes on the bottom plate. Adjust the position of the balance so that it is parallel with the bottom plate, and then carefully press the balance cock down onto the bottom plate, at the same time making sure that the top pivot of the balance engages with the pivot hole in the balance cock. Give the movement a gentle shake to set the balance oscillating. If the balance swings freely, press the balance cock fully home and fit its retaining screw and tighten it, all the time checking that the balance remains free to oscillate. Check that the regulator pins are either side of the outer turn of the balance spring and, if not, carefully move the balance spring until correctly positioned.

### Half and Three-Quarter Plate Movements – Balance Spring Fixed to the Balance Cock

123 Balance and balance cock with balance spring fixed to stud on the balance cock.

If the balance spring is fixed to the balance cock (not so common), turn the balance cock upside-down and place the balance on the cock. Feed the end of the balance spring through the stud on the balance cock and adjust the position of the balance spring until the impulse jewel is roughly in a position so that when it engages with the fork of the lever, the lever sits mid-way between the banking pins (this can be adjusted later once the balance has been fitted). Pin the balance spring in place with a tapered brass pin. Carefully turn the balance cock over; try not to let the balance dangle on the balance spring. Lower the balance cock onto the movement and position the lower pivot of the balance into its pivot hole. Engage the steady pins on the balance cock with their corresponding holes on the bottom plate. Adjust the position of the balance so that it is parallel with the bottom plate, then carefully press the balance cock down onto the bottom plate, at the same time making sure that the top pivot of the balance engages with its pivot hole. Give the movement a gentle shake to set the balance oscillating. If the balance swings freely, press the balance cock fully home and fit its retaining screw and tighten it. Check that the regulator pins are either side of the outer turn of the balance spring. If not, carefully move the balance spring until correctly positioned.

Once the balance has stopped oscillating, check that the lever is mid-way between the banking pins. If the lever is not central between the banking pins, remove the balance cock and tapered brass pin and adjust the balance spring's position, feeding more of the balance spring through the stud to move the lever to the right, or pull the balance spring back to move the lever to the left. Replace the balance cock and check that the lever is now central between the banking pins and, if necessary, repeat the above until it is.

## Winding the Watch

The movement has now been fully assembled and is ready to be wound; using the correct sized key, slowly wind it up, keeping an eye on the fusee to make sure that, as the fusee chain reaches the top of the fusee, the fusee chain engages the stop iron. If the stop is working correctly, it should prevent you from winding any further. The watch is now fully wound and, if all has gone well, the watch should start ticking (it may require a slight shake to get it going).

Once you are happy that the movement is running well, holding the movement with the bottom plate uppermost, fit the motion work and dial washer (if required). Then fit the dial and retaining pins. Fit the dust cap, if the movement has one. Support the movement in a movement holder face up and fit the hands. First fit the second hand and press into place with a case knife or similar (do not use your finger), making sure that it is level and that it does not drag on the dial.

## Fitting the Hands (Front-Set Hands)

Loosely fit the minute hand to the cannon pinion and adjust the cannon pinion so that the minute hand is aligned to 12

124 Hands fitted to a front-set movement.

o'clock. Remove the minute hand and fit the hour hand so that it points to 12 o'clock. Press it into place and check that it is parallel to the dial. Refit the minute hand (pointing to 12 o'clock) and press into place on the cannon pinion.

## Fitting the Hands (Rear-Set Hands)

125 Hands fitting to a rear-set movement.

Fit the hour hand and press it into place. Using a key, rotate the hand setting arbor until the hour hand is pointing to 12 o'clock. Place the minute hand on the cannon pinion; place the movement on a staking tool with the hand setting arbor on a flat area (away from any holes). Use a hollow punch with a hole just larger that the diameter of the cannon pinion, tap the minute hand onto the cannon pinion.

## Checking the Hands

Check that the minute and hour hands are level. Rotate the hands through a full twelve hours to make sure they do not catch. If all is well, set the hands to the correct time and put the watch to one side for twenty-four hours and then check that it is keeping time correctly.

## It Runs Until the End of the Wind

The movement runs until the mainspring has run down. This is the desired result of all your hard work. For a watch to be considered working, it should run for more than twenty-four hours (typically thirty hours) on a full wind. It should also keep good time (after adjustment of the regulator), which is within plus or minus two minutes in twenty-four hours, although better accuracy can usually be obtained with careful adjustment of the regulator. The results when the watch is carried around may not be quite so good.

# The Watch Will Not Run

L ike all mechanical devices, watches do not always work as intended. This may be owing to any number of reasons, such as a damaged or badly fitted part, too much friction in the train or any number of other problems that may prevent it from working properly.

## If the Balance Does Not Swing Freely

- Check that the balance spring is level and not catching on the top plate (if fitted under the balance), the underside of the balance cock (if fitted above the balance) or on the balance itself.

- Make sure that the balance spring is symmetrical with respect to the balance staff (it should spiral out from the centre evenly when viewed from above).

- Check that the balance pivot holes are clean and undamaged.

- Are the pivots smooth? If not, burnish them using a Jacot tool (*see* the chapter 'Broken Balance Pivot' for details).

- Check that the safety pin on the lever is not rubbing on the edge of the table roller. If it is, remove the lever and carefully bend it back. It is important that you do not bend it back too far, otherwise it will not be able to perform its correct function (*see* section on 'Lever Safety Action').

- Check the escape wheel's teeth: are any bent or distorted? If yes, remove the escape wheel and straighten by holding a pair of tweezers at the base of the spur and, while keeping light pressure on the tweezers, slide them towards the tip.

- A sluggish train may be caused by a distorted top plate, bottom plate or third-wheel bridge. Do all the wheels have the correct end shake? If not, check that both the top and bottom plates are flat; if either plate is found to be distorted, it needs to be flattened. You can straighten the distorted plate by applying a small amount of pressure in the opposite direction to the distortion. Reassemble and check if the train is free-running.

- A lack of power to the lever. Remove the balance cock and balance, and then, using a piece of sharpened peg wood, carefully move the lever from side to side. If the lever is moved a small amount (1–2mm), it should snap back when you let go (owing to draw). If you move the lever a bit more, it should snap over to the other side and the escape wheel rotate by one tooth. If this does not happen, the problem may well be in the train. Let down the tension in the mainspring and check that all the wheels have a small amount of end shake, which means that they can move up and down between the plates by a small amount. If one of the wheels does not have enough end shake, it might be because it is being pinched between the top and bottom plate or by the third-wheel bridge. Disassemble the movement and reassemble it without the lever, then wind it up a little and see if the escape wheel rotates freely. Do not wind more than a couple of 'clicks' as running the train at high speed may damage the pivots, especially those of the escape wheel. If it does not run freely, then remove first the escape wheel and repeat, then remove the fourth and try again. Look closely at the wheels you remove and check for any dirt, distortion or bent pivots. If all looks well after checking, reassemble and check again for free running.

126 Inserting a small piece of paper under the third-wheel bridge to lift it up slightly.

127 Increasing the end shake on the centre wheel using a Rose cutter.

If the problem is the third-wheel bridge, then placing a small piece of paper between it and the bottom plate before tightening the retaining screws can raise the bridge very slightly and might cure the problem.

If the problem is that one of the other wheels or the lever has insufficient end shake, this can be rectified using a rose cutter to remove a small amount of brass from the underside of the top or bottom plate.

Choose a cutter whose diameter is just larger than the diameter of the arbor and only remove a very small amount of metal; reassemble and test for end shake. Repeat the above until there is sufficient end shake.

- The watch stops with both hands in line. This is a classic problem usually caused by one of the hands catching on the other. Check from the side with a loupe and lift the offending hand clear with tweezers. The watch can also be stopped if the hour hand catches on the second hand. Check also that the minute hand is not in contact with the watch glass when the front bezel is closed, as this can slow or stop a watch as well.

- The movement runs well when in the case but stops when you close the front bezel. This is often caused by pressure on the balance cock as a result of the inner back of the case having become pushed in. Remove the movement and, using your thumbs, press the inner rear back slightly outwards.

- The watch only works face down. The balance may be catching on the jewel-mounting screws on the balance cock. If the screws protrude below the underside of the balance cock, remove the screws and file down the end a bit, screw them back into the balance cock and check that they are flush with the underside.

- The balance is too tight. This may be the case if the balance cock has become distorted and is pressing down on the pivots. To check whether this is the problem, slightly undo the screw holding the balance cock in place. If the balance now swings freely, then you will need to adjust the balance cock. To raise the balance cock, place a small piece of paper or tin foil under the balance cock foot before screwing in place.

- The lever pallets unlock incorrectly. As the balance moves backwards and forwards, the impulse jewel moves the lever first one way then the other. It is stopped from moving too far by the banking pins (one either side of the lever). The position of these is crucial to the correct operation of the watch. If they are bent too far towards the lever, the pallets will not unlock the escape-wheel teeth. If they are too far apart, the pallets may interfere with the escape wheel. The impulse jewel may also be unable to engage with the lever fork so preventing energy being transferred to the balance. The banking pins are either on the underside of the top plate for a full plate movement or on the bottom plate for half and three-quarter plate movements. They can be in front of, or behind, the lever pivot (more commonly behind). The banking pins can easily be adjusted by bending them towards or away from the lever. Depending on where the banking pins are positioned, you may need to remove the balance in order to make adjustments. With the movement wound up, move the lever from one side to the other with a piece of peg wood; it should snap over and the escape-wheel tooth should disengage and the escape wheel should rotate a small amount, and the opposite lever pallet should engage with the next tooth on the escape wheel. Flipping the lever back the other way should repeat the cycle. In all cases, the pins need to be adjusted so that the lever pallet just unlocks from the escape-wheel tooth. Try and keep the position of both banking pins symmetrical as well.

- A weak mainspring may cause a sluggish balance. First check that the balance swings freely with the spring fully unwound. If the balance does swing freely, first apply a bit more setup to the mainspring and see if that cures the problem. If increasing the setup does not fix the problem, try replacing the mainspring with a stronger one. Be careful not to fit one that is too strong, as this may damage the movement. Before changing the spring, make sure you have checked for free running of the train; the problem could be binding pivots on the wheels, etc.

- The watch runs for thirty minutes or so than stops. One possible cause of this may be an overly tight-fitting main-spring. If you let down the tension in the mainspring (*see* the chapter 'Dismantling a Watch' for details of how this is done), does the fusee chain unwind smoothly onto the barrel? If not, this might be due to the mainspring catching on the inside of the barrel. Remove the mainspring from the barrel and check if the internal surfaces are smooth and flat; if not, remove any roughness. Any unevenness can be removed using a flat-ended punch and stake. Place the barrel on the staking tool and lightly tap the end of the punch to flatten any bumps. If this does not cure the problem, it might be necessary to replace the mainspring with one with a slightly reduced height, but having a similar strength.

## Incorrect Parts Fitted

Do not assume that all the parts found in a movement are original to that movement. It is quite possible that someone in the past has replaced a damaged or missing part in order to try to get the watch to work. This may not have been successful. The replacement part may, therefore, be the cause of the movement not working.

## Tight-Fitting Hour Wheel

Pushing the hour hand on to the hour wheel can sometimes cause the hour wheel pipe to distort. This in turn can cause the hour wheel to grip the cannon pinion too tightly, which often causes the watch to run slowly or stop. To fix this problem, with the hour wheel removed from the cannon pinion, push the hour hand on to the hour wheel and then very carefully run a cutting broach around the inside of the hour wheel pipe (only hold the hour wheel, not the hand, because there is a high risk of breaking the hand off). Place the hour wheel over the cannon pinion and check that it can rotate freely. Repeat, if necessary, until the hour wheel rotates freely on the cannon pinion.

## Damaged or Worn Pivot Hole

If a pivot hole has become enlarged owing to wear (this only applies to pivot holes that are drilled directly in the plates, not jewelled ones that can be fixed by replacing the worn jewel), it can be fixed by inserting a new bush. This consists of a small brass tube whose sides are very slightly sloped and with a hole drilled down the centre. The old pivot hole must first be enlarged so that the new bush can be fitted. Use a cutting broach, and working from the inside, open the hole until the front of the bush just fits the hole. While enlarging the hole, make sure that the cutting broach is kept perpendicular to the plate. The broach should have produced a slightly conical hole in the plate. To fit the bush, first place the plate (inner surface uppermost) on the table of a staking tool with the pivot hole over an opening on the staking tool. The bush is then fitted in place by positioning the front in the hole and, using a flat-faced punch, tapped into place. Once you are happy that it is correctly

128 Using a flat-faced punch to tap a new bush into place.

positioned, remove any of the bush that protrudes either side of the plate using a suitably sized rose cutter. Then, using a cutting broach, open the pivot hole until the pivot fits. Finally, finish the hole with a smoothing broach.

## Repairing a Bent Pivot

Sometimes you will find that the pivot on a wheel or other part has become bent; this needs to be straightened before the watch will work properly. Great care is needed to prevent the pivot from breaking off. You need to use pliers with brass-faced jaws. The end of the jaws should be gently warmed over a spirit lamp or gas stove flame. Holding the wheel between the thumb and finger, close the jaws of the heated pliers over the bent pivot (do not close too firmly) and at the same time carefully pull away from the pivot. This action may need to be repeated a few times until the pivot is straight (each time warming the pliers). No matter how careful you are, in some cases the pivot will break off. For this reason, it is worth trying this technique on scrap wheels before you try it on a wheel from a good watch.

## Bent or Misaligned Balance

Sometimes, the balance can become bent or distorted owing to heavy handling (this is particularly true of cut balances). It is fairly easy to re-align the balance, holding it with pliers and pulling or pushing the bent section back into place. You are aiming to return the balance to as near a perfect circle as possible, while also keeping it flat in the horizontal plane. Although not specifically designed for the purpose, a depthing tool can be used to check on how successful you have been in returning a balance to an original shape. Fit the balance on to the depthing tool and then spin the balance and watch for how much it wobbles. Try and make adjustments until it stops wobbling when spun.

129 A balance mounted in a depth tool to check wobble, after repair.

## Broken Balance Pivot

One of the more common faults encountered in watch repair work is a broken balance pivot, which is often the result of a watch having been dropped. There is little that can be done to repair the original balance pivot; the only solution is to replace the damaged balance staff.

## Disassembly When the Balance Spring is Below the Balance

130 Removing the table roller from a balance.

First, you need to remove the table roller, but before you do, make a note of where it sits so you can replace it in the same position. Using brass-faced pliers, grip the edges of the table roller and, with a twisting action, gentle pull the table roller away from the balance. Be very careful, as it is easy to slip and break the impulse jewel. Once free, place it in a storage tray.

Slide the blade of a craft knife under the balance spring collet and lever it up until it comes free. Lift the balance spring away from the balance assembly and place in a storage tray.

## Disassembly When the Balance Spring is Above the Balance

The process is the same as when the balance spring is mounted under the balance, except that you need to remove the balance spring first, then remove the table roller.

On most fusee lever watches the balance staff is made of polished steel fitted into a brass collar. The collar has a turned shoulder, which is a tight fit on to the balance. To remove the damaged balance staff, place the balance assembly over a hole on a staking tool table just large than the diameter of the brass collar. With a suitably sized hollow punch, push out the balance staff and brass collar.

You can then either make, or have made, a new balance staff. Making a new balance staff requires skill in using a lathe, which is beyond the scope of this book. In fact I am not sure that it is possible to learn how to turn a part

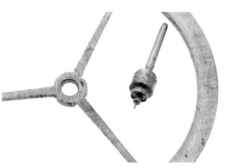

131 Balance staff, with broken pivots, removed from a balance.

from a book. To truly learn this skill you need to find a course that can teach the practical skills needed to master the lathe. The BHI (*see* Appendix I for contact details) run such courses, or there may be other courses offered at your local college.

An alternative to making a new balance staff is to take a good balance staff from a broken watch movement. The new balance staff needs to be exactly the same overall length and similar diameter to the original. You might also need to adjust the position of the brass collar to make sure that the balance is at the same height as the original. If the hole in the balance is too small for the brass collar, it can be enlarged with a cutting broach; the fit should be a tight one. Put the balance staff in place and put the assembly on the staking tool. Using a hollow punch, lightly tap the staff into place. Try the balance assembly by placing it between the balance cock and bottom pivot hole, checking that it is perpendicular and that when the balance assemble is rotated, the balance remains true (i.e. does not wobble). It should also run freely and take several seconds to come to a stop. Also check that the balance clears any other part fitted under the balance, such as the regulator.

If the pivots on the replacement balance staff are too large for the pivot holes, this can be rectified using a set of turns, like a small hand-driven lathe. Use the gauge to establish the

132 Balance fitted on a set of turns.

correct size for the pivot by measuring the old balance staff. If both ends are broken, you will need to try the pivot at each stage until it fits. Select a runner that is just smaller than the current size of the pivot. Do not go straight to the final size as this could put too much stress on the pivot and it may break off. Place the balance on the turns and adjust its position by moving the runner bar in and out until the pivot just rests in the runner, and then lock it in position. Lightly hold an Arkansas stone over the pivot resting on the tool and then, using the bow, slowly rotate the balance, keeping light pressure on the stone. Do this until the balance pivot cannot be reduced any further. Lift the balance away and unlock the runner bar, then rotate this to the next position and set up as before. Repeat this until the new pivot is the same size as the original pivot. Repeat for the other end.

133 Balance fitted on to a Jacot tool.

When both pivots are the right size, fit them in a Jacot tool and burnish the pivots. Choose a suitably sized runner: the gauge that comes with the Jacot tool will tell you what size to use. Place the pivot on the runner and engage the drive and slowly rotate with the bow while moving the burnishing tool across the pivot. Try it in the watch and check that it spins freely (check in all orientations of the movement).

Assuming that it is spinning freely, reassemble the rest of the balance. Place the balance on a staking tool with the bottom pivot uppermost (you will need to use a stand-off to prevent the balance from becoming

134 Refitting balance spring.

distorted). For balances with the balance spring mounted underneath the balance, place the balance spring collet over the balance staff (make sure the balance spring is the correct way round, spiralling inwards in a clockwise direction, viewed from the top). Using a suitably sized hollow staking tool push the collet over the brass collar and lightly tap it down as far as it will go.

Fit the table roller using the correct staking tool (this is a modified hollow stake with a groove cut in one side to accommodate the impulse jewel) and carefully tap it into position on the balance staff. For ease of fitting the

135 Refitting table roller.

balance on to the movement later, I always align the position of the impulse jewel with one of the support struts on the balance. You may also need to rotate the balance spring so that it is in the right position for its mounting stud.

Fit the complete assembly on to the movement. If all has gone well, the balance should oscillate freely for a few seconds when shaken.

Fit the lever and check that the table roller clears it. With the movement held with the balance uppermost, there should be approximately 1mm of clearance between the upper surface of the lever and the lower surface of the table roller.

## A Broken Pivot on a Wheel

If you find a wheel with a broken pivot, there are a number of ways that this can be fixed:

- One way is to use a replacement wheel from a scrap watch. For this to be successful, the wheel diameter, pinion length and number of teeth must all be identical; the distance between the pivots must also be of the same length or it will not fit between the plates.

- The second method is to remove the arbor from the wheel and replace it with a good one. Again the arbor must be the same size and the pinion must have the same number of teeth as the damaged, original one. The arbor is fixed to the wheel by a friction fit. To remove it, place the wheel on a staking tool with the arbor through a hole a little larger than its diameter. Then, using a suitable punch, tap the arbor until it drops away from the wheel. The new arbor is fitted in place by turning the wheel over and placing it above a smaller hole (just bigger than the diameter of the new arbor) and using a suitable punch; lightly tap it until the new arbor is flush with the wheel. It is very important to make sure that the arbor is perpendicular to the wheel.

136 Removing damaged arbor from a wheel.

- A third way is to first remove the wheel from the arbor, then heat the broken end of the arbor in a spirit lamp or gas stove flame until it turns fully red in colour and then allow it to cool slowly. This tempers the steel, making it possible to drill into the end. Care must be taken not to overheat the part. The next bit is quite tricky, as you need to drill a small hole, about 3mm deep, into the end of the arbor where the broken pivot used to be. Note that there is a special tool that is designed to help with drilling the hole (called a watchmaker's pivoting tool). Once the hole has been drilled, place the wheel on the table of the staking tool and fit a length of blued steel wire, about 6mm long, into the hole. Using a flat-face stake, tap the length of blued steel home. The diameter of the hole is dependent on the diameter of the blued steel wire, and should be sized to give a tight fit. Once you are happy with the new pivot, it needs to be reduced to the correct size using a set of turns and then burnished on a Jacot tool (as described in the chapter 'Broken Balance Pivot').

137 Drilling a hole in an arbor to repair a broken pivot, using pivoting tool.

## A Broken Impulse Jewel

To replace a broken impulse jewel, you first need to remove the remains of the old one. The impulse jewel is usually held in place with shellac. First, carefully remove the impulse roller as described in the chapter 'Broken Balance Pivot' (noting its position on the balance staff). Using a sharp metal point (the end of a broach or something similar), push out the remains of the old jewel and shellac; make sure the hole is clear of any old shellac. Choose a new impulse jewel of the same size and check that it fits the hole correctly; also check that it is the correct size for the lever forks. Place the table roller in a pin vice (vertically), fit the impulse jewel in place with the top of the impulse jewel flush with top of the table roller; also make sure that the flat surface faces forward, and fix it in place with shellac applied to the top of the impulse jewel. To get the shellac to melt, you will need to apply a small amount of heat. Use the heated end of a piece of brass wire 1mm in diameter to provide this. Check that the impulse jewel is at right angles to the table; if not, adjust by warming the shellac and moving the impulse jewel with tweezers. Replace the table roller on the balance staff and fit in place as detailed in the chapter 'Broken Balance Pivot'.

## Missing Teeth on a Wheel

Missing teeth on a wheel can be repaired as follows: using a suitably sized needle file, remove the section with the damaged teeth, leaving a slot with sloping sides. Cut a piece of brass just slightly thicker than the wheel and file it to fit the slot already cut in the wheel. Soft solder the patch in place with a soldering iron and then, using a needle file, form new teeth to match the

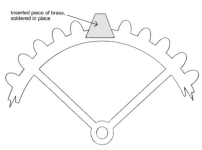

original ones. When you are happy with the new teeth, use an Arkansas stone to reduce the thickness of the patch to match the rest of the wheel. Use steel wool to smooth the edges of the teeth. Test

138 Replacing the missing teeth on a wheel.

that the new teeth mesh smoothly with the leaves of the next wheel and adjust accordingly.

## A Loose or Slipping Cannon Pinion

A watch can appear sometimes to run well, but keeps very poor time or the hands stop moving altogether. This is often caused by a loose or slipping cannon pinion. To fix this, remove the hands, dial and motion work. Check the cannon pinion; it should be able to rotate on the centre wheel arbor, but there should be enough resistance to prevent the cannon pinion from slipping. If the cannon pinion is too loose, the centre wheel cannot turn the cannon pinion and hence the hands. If the cannon pinion has a dimple on the side (not common on fusee lever watches), you can use the following method, for which there is a special tool, resembling a miniature staking tool. The cannon pinion is placed on the tool and rotated until the dimple is uppermost. The small punch is then brought down until it is in contact with the cannon pinion with the end resting neatly in the dimple. Give the punch a light tap. Re-fit the cannon pinion and test it for tightness; repeat until the cannon pinion feels tight enough.

139 Tightening a loose cannon pinion.

If the cannon pinion does not have a dimple on the side, then you need to use the following method to stop the cannon pinion from slipping. Remove the cannon pinion from the centre wheel arbor and, using a pair of end cutters, lightly grip the centre wheel arbor a few millimetres from the bottom (close to the bottom plate). Rotate the cutters while maintaining light pressure; this should score the surface of the centre wheel arbor, leaving a very slightly raised area. Repeat this a couple of times, each time moving the cutters up the arbor a few millimetres. Be careful not to apply too much pressure to the cutters, as there is a danger that you might cut through the centre wheel arbor. It might be best to practise on a redundant centre wheel arbor before carrying out this adjustment on a working movement. Refit the cannon pinion and test it for tightness; repeat as required until the cannon pinion feels tight enough.

## Loose Pillars

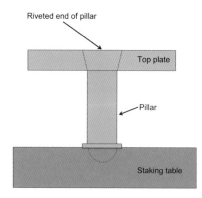

Riveted end of pillar

Top plate

Pillar

Staking table

140 Re-riveting a loose pillar.

The pillars that hold the top and bottom plates together are riveted into the top plate. On dismantling a movement, it may be found that some of the pillars are loose. To fix this problem, put the rounded end of the pillar into a hole on the staking tool table, just bigger than the top of the pillar but small enough for the flange to rest on the top of the staking table. Using a round-ended punch, lightly tap the centre of the pillar where it comes through the top plate, until the pillar is firm.

This process can also be applied to a dial plate, but because the dial plate does not have a flange that can rest on the staking tool, you need to protect the fixing holes from closing up by fitting smoothing broaches through the hole.

## Listening to the Watch

A lot can be gained by listening to the ticking of a pocket watch: a lever movement should have a clear tick (caused by the end of the lever hitting the banking pins); there should be a slight metallic ring. If the sound is not a clear tick, it may indicate that something is not quite right. After listening to a few watches you will get an idea of what a good watch sounds like and whether or not there is a problem. The sort of things to listen out for are the sound of the balance spring rubbing on the balance or balance cock (which produces a slight rasping sound), or the edge of the balance catching on the underside of the balance cock or other part of the watch.

Remember to listen to the watch in a number of different orientations.

## When to Give Up!

No matter how experienced you become, there will still be times when a particular problem defeats you. When this happens, the best thing to do is to put the watch to one side (make sure you keep all the bits together and record the work you have already carried out) and try again in a few weeks' time. You will be surprised how an apparently insoluble problem suddenly becomes straightforward. This may be owing to the fact that your skills have improved or that a fresh look at the problem has given you a new insight. Remember, watch repairing should be a pleasure, not an obsession!

# Dating a Watch

All English fusee lever watches, which are cased in silver or gold, will have hallmarks (a legal requirement); from these it is possible to date the watch (*see* Appendix I for websites that list hallmarks). Additional information as to the age of a watch can be gained from the case maker's initials, if present (see *Watch Case Makers of England* by Philip T. Priestley for more information). The style of the case and dial can also be used to give an approximate idea of the date. The watchmaker's name can also be used to give an approximate age for the watch. *Watchmakers and Clockmakers of the World* by Brian Looms gives details of more than 70,000 watch and clockmakers with the dates of when they were working.

Be careful when dating a watch from the hallmarks, as the sequence of date letters are repeated and it is all too easy to get carried away and attribute a much earlier date to your watch than it really has. For instance, the sequence for London hallmarks for the years 1776–95 and 1816–35 look much the same, so you need to use other information, such as the maker's name, case style and case maker's initials, to corroborate the hallmark date.

## A Marriage

There can sometimes be a problem with relying on the hallmarks alone to date a watch. This is because the movement may not be original to the case, which is known as a 'marriage', and may have occurred for legitimate reasons, for example the case may have become worn and have been replaced with a new custom-made one. If the watchcase and movement have serial numbers, and they match, this is a good indication that the case and movement started life together. If, however, the serial numbers do not match, then you may well be looking at a marriage. Other indications that the movement is not original to the case include the winding hole not truly aligning with the winding square or the case having been modified so they do. Another indicator that you have a marriage is the movement catch not correctly engaging with the case.

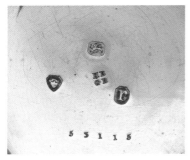

141 London hallmark for 1832, the case maker's name is Horatio & George Elliot Bartlett.

142 Chester hallmark for 1894, the case maker's name is Samuel Yeomans.

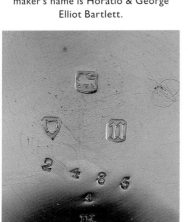

143 London hallmark for 1868, the case maker's name is John William Hammon.

# Selling Pocket Watches

If you are a collector of pocket watches, then the need to repair a watch is an end in itself. However, you may want to consider selling watches as either a way of making money or to subsidize your collecting. Any watch that can be described as working, and by that I mean able to run with reasonable accuracy and for at least twenty-four hours between windings, will always fetch a higher price than one that is not in working order. You may wish to sell to an antique dealer or shop, but be aware that the price you receive will be a lot lower than the retail sale price that you see in the shop window. This is because the retailer has to cover their overheads (rent, lighting, heating, and so on) and be able to make a profit. They may also have to carry stock for quite a long time before it sells.

An alternative to selling via a shop is to use some form of auction. There are two types: the more traditional auction house and the online auction. With the traditional auction house, you hand over the watch to them and they are responsible for describing the item, printing the catalogue, running the auction and collecting the money from the buyer. For this service they charge you, and with the larger companies, the buyer as well, a fee based on a percentage of the final sale price. Unless it is a fairly valuable watch, it probably is not worth considering this route. For lower value watches (and even some more valuable ones), it might be better to use an online auction site. The best known is probably eBay, but there are others who deal with pocket watches, and they all operate in much the same way. You are responsible for listing the item, collecting payment and posting the item to the purchaser. You will be charged a fee for both listing the item (even if it does not sell) and a final value fee, based on a percentage of the sale price. There may be other costs, depending on the payment method you choose. The advantage of an online auction is that you are in full control, setting the start price and how it is described and so on. To get the best price, you need to provide a good, detailed description and high-quality photographs. These need to show more than one view and must include the movement. Try to be honest about your watch; make sure you mention faults as well as the good points. Remember, a satisfied customer will come back time and again but a dissatisfied one will tell everybody to stay away from you.

Your potential market is worldwide and there are a large number of very knowledgeable collectors who will pick up on a good or unusual watch.

It is best not to start by selling valuable watches until you have built up a reputation. Once you are established, you may consider selling more valuable watches. Look at other people's listings to get an idea of what sells and what does not. Also, you can gain useful information by looking at other sellers' listing, but do not copy from other people's auctions.

# Appendix I

## Sources of Information and Suppliers

**www.925-1000.com**
Online encyclopedia of silver hallmarks from around the world, with very good section on UK hallmarks.

**www.agthomas.co.uk**
Horological and jewellery supplies.

**www.ahsoc.org**
Antiquarian Horological Society, founded in 1953 and dedicated to the study of clocks and watches from a historical point of view.

**www.antique-watch.com**
Pieces of Time, good source of high quality pocket watches with a useful photographic index.

**www.bhi.co.uk**
The British Horological Institute, a very good source of technical information plus links to many other useful sites.

**www.cousinsuk.com**
Cousins UK, UK supplier of watch and clock parts.

**www.ebay.co.uk**
Good site to buy and sell pocket watches plus tools and materials.

**www.home.datacomm.ch/rbu/index.html**
Useful A–Z of watch and clock terms.

**www.hswalsh.com**
A UK company, watch materials and tools plus a very useful dial repair kit.

**www.nawcc.org**
National Association of Watch and Clock Collectors (USA), a very good site with a vast amount of information, including a very comprehensive list of museums with watch and clock collections and a great section showing animated escapements.

**www.oldandsold.com/articles02/clocks-a.shtml**
Very helpful and comprehensive encyclopaedia of clock and watch terminology.

**www.rnhorological.co.uk**
A UK company with a very large range of tools and materials for both clocks and watches (fast delivery).

**www.tickintimeworldofwatchtools.co.uk**
Good range of tools.

# Appendix II

## Further Reading

Betts, J., *Time Restored* (Oxford University Press, 2006). Details the long and often difficult journey that Lt Cdr R. T. Gould took in his quest to repair and restore John Harrison's timekeepers (H1 to H5). This is a very well researched and detailed biography of Gould, covering his whole life and giving a fascinating insight into what drove him to dedicate a large part of it to Harrison's timekeepers.

Britten, F. J., *Britten's Old Clocks and Watches and Their Makers* (Bloomsbury Books, 1986). This book contains a great deal of useful information, including a list of clock- and watchmakers. It has been revised and reprinted many times; the current one is the 9th edition.

Britten, F. J., *Britten's Watch & Clock Maker's Handbook, Dictionary and Guide*, 16th edition (Methuen, 1978; reprinted Bloomsbury Books, 1987). Contains a large amount of very useful information on watches and clocks, with excellent illustrations.

Camerer Cuss, T. P., *The Story of Watches* (MacGibbon and Kee Ltd and The Philosophical Library, 1952). Interesting account of the development of the pocket watch with black and white photos. Now out of print but you should be able to track down a second-hand copy.

Chamberlain, P., *It's About Time* (Holland Press, 1978). Deals with the more unusual movements that developed after the verge; also has a very good biographical section covering early watchmakers.

Clutton, C. and Daniels, G., *Watches*, 3rd edition (Sotheby Parke Bernet Publications, 1979). Detailed and very well-illustrated history of the pocket watch from 1500 to the modern day.

Cutmore, M., *The Pocket Watch Handbook* (David & Charles Publishers, 2002). A very useful and well-written introduction to the pocket watch.

Daniels, G., *Watchmaking* (Sotheby's Publications and Philip Wilson Publishers, 1985). George Daniels designed and made pocket watches; he manufactured every part, including the dial and case. This is a superb book covering the whole process from start to finish and is, therefore, a great source of information if you need to make a replacement part yourself or just want to understand how a pocket watch is designed and made.

Daniels, G., *'All In Good Time' Reflections of a Watchmaker* (Daniels, 2006). This autobiography covers all of his life, detailing how he became fascinated by watches, ultimately leading him to becoming one of the greatest watchmakers of all time.

De Carle, D., *Practical Watch Repairing*, 3rd edition (N.A.G Press Ltd, 2006). Although this book mostly covers the more modern, machine-made watch, there is a useful section on the English fusee lever.

De Carle, D., *Watch & Clock Encyclopaedia*, 3rd edition (N.A.G. Press, 1983). A very useful and well-illustrated encyclopedia of horological terms.

Garrard, F. J., *Watch Repairing, Cleaning and Adjusting* (Crosby Lockwood and Son, 1922). Very using and practical book, now sadly out of print.

Gazeley, W. J., *Clock and Watch Escapements* (Robert Hale, 1992). Detailed and quite technical discussion of clock and watch escapements. The book covers most of the escapements you are likely to encounter.

Jagger, C., *The World's Great Clocks & Watches* (Galley Press, 1977). Very well-illustrated book covering all aspects of timekeeping from sundials and water clocks through to the very complicated clocks and watches of the late nineteenth century. A greater emphasis is given to clocks than watches.

Kemp, R., *The Englishman's Watch* (John Sherratt and Son Ltd, 1979). A lively and well written account of an amateur watch collector's collection, covering the ordinary and workday watches that the collector is more likely to come across, although it covers other watch escapements as well; there is a good section on the English fusee lever.

Kemp, R., *The Fusee Lever Watch* (John Sherratt and Son Ltd, 1981). A very good account of the development of the English fusee lever pocket watch.

Loomes, B., *Watchmakers and Clockmakers of the World* (N.A.G. Press, 2006). This contains the details of 70,000 clock and watchmakers from around the world, listing when and where they worked.

Priestley, P. T., *Watch Case Makers of England* (National Association of Watch and Clock Collectors, 1994). This is an American publication, which includes a wealth of information regarding watchcase manufacture in England, plus a list of makers in and around the three main areas of production (London, Birmingham and Chester).

Treherne, T., *The Massey Family – Clock, Watch, Chronometer and Nautical Instrument Makers* (Newcastle-under-Lyme Museum, 1977). Catalogue of an exhibition held at Newcastle-under-Lyme borough museum, drawing together lots of useful information on the Massey family.

Various Authors, *Pioneers of Precision Timekeeping* (The Antiquarian Horological Society). A collection of articles original published in the *Antiquarian Horology*, the quarterly publication of the Antiquarian Horology Society. The articles give a fascinating insight into the development of precision timekeeping, including an article on Mudge's first lever watch.

Weiss, L., *Watch-Making in England 1760–1820* (Robert Hale, 1982). Very well researched and written; a fascinating account of the English watch trade during the reign of George III, detailing all the operations needed to produce a finished watch. This book gives a good insight into the way watches were made before the advent of the machine-made watch.

White, A., *The Chain Makers* (Hampshire County Council Museum Service and Christchurch Local History Society, 2000). The area around Christchurch, Hampshire became the centre of English fusee chain manufacture in the late eighteenth century and early nineteenth century and this short account gives a fascinating insight into this industry.

Whiten, A.J., *Repairing Old Clocks and Watches* (Robert Hale, 1979). Well illustrated with very clear line drawings; covers watches (pocket and wrist) and clocks.

# Appendix III

## Some Useful Terms

**Arbor** – Axle or shaft on which a wheel or pinion is mounted. When referring to pallets or balance, the arbor is called a staff.

**Balance cock** – This forms the upper pivot of the balance and either partly or fully covers the balance. In early watches this was elaborately pierced and engraved, during the nineteenth century it became smaller (only partly covering the balance) and usually only engraved, sometimes being completely plain. The balance cock can also carry the regulator.

**Balance screws** – A series of screws set around the rim of the balance, used to adjust the timing of the balance.

**Balance spring** – Also known as a hairspring (American). The fine-coiled spring fitted to the balance, which causes the balance to oscillate when acted on by the escapement. The effective length of the spring determines the rate at which the balance oscillates.

**Balance spring collet** – Split brass ring attached to the inner end of the balance spring. The collet is a frictional fit on the balance staff.

**Balance spring stud** – Stud mounted on the top plate through which the outer end of the balance spring is secured via a tapered brass pin.

**Banking pins** – A pair of pins set either side of the lever and positioned so that when the lever is at rest it is against one or other of the banking pins.

**Barrel** – Also known as the mainspring barrel, the drum-shaped container that holds the mainspring.

**Barrel arbor** – The axis on which the barrel rotates. The barrel arbor has a hook, which engages with the inner end of the mainspring.

**Barrel bridge** – A bridge that fits over the barrel and supports one end of the barrel arbor.

**Bottom plate** – Sometimes called the dial plate, the plate on which the dial is mounted, also carries the pillars to which the top plate is attached.

**Bow** – Loop of metal attached to the pendant used for fixing onto a watch chain.

**Cannon pinion** – The pinion on to which the minute hand is usually fitted. It is a friction fit onto the centre wheel arbor or hand setting arbor on half and three-quarter plate movements.

**Centre wheel and pinion** – As the name implies, the wheel at the centre of the watch. Also known as the second wheel, it carries an extended arbor on which the cannon pinion fits (on full plate movements). The centre wheel is driven from the great wheel on the fusee.

**Cylinder escapement** – A type of frictional rest escapement designed by George Graham (1675–1751) in 1725. It was never very popular in England and only found on a few high-end watches. Later it became the most common type of escapement employed by Swiss and French watchmakers during the nineteenth century and early twentieth century.

**Detached lever** – A type of escapement independently designed by Thomas Mudge (1715–94) and Julien LeRoy (1686–1759) in which impulse to the balance is only given for a small fraction of the total time the balance is in motion. This reduces the friction on the balance and hence improves the accuracy of the watch.

**Detent** – A click or pawl, most often associated with the fusee maintaining-power ratchet.

**Dial plate** – A metal (usually brass) plate on to which the dial is mounted. The dial plate is then fixed to the top plate with brass pins.

**Dial washer** – A thin washer, usually brass, that fits over the hour wheel of the motion work and presses lightly on the underside of the dial to help keep the motion work in place.

**Draw** – The force that keeps the lever held against the banking pins, even if the movement is subject to a jolt. Draw is achieved by the relative angle of the lever pallets in relation to the escape wheel teeth.

**Duplex escapement** – A form of frictional rest escapement conceived by Dutertre in about 1720 then modified by Thomas Tyrer in 1782. The escape wheel has two rows of teeth, one short and one long. One of the longer teeth rests on the balance staff as it rotates; the tooth eventually drops through a notch in the staff as it rotates and as it does so, one of the short teeth on the escape wheel engages with a pallet on the balance staff and gives it a 'kick'.

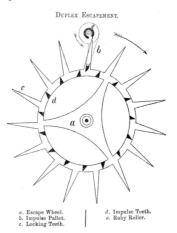

DUPLEX ESCAPEMENT.

a. Escape Wheel.
b. Impulse Pallet.
c. Locking Teeth.

d. Impulse Teeth.
e. Ruby Roller.

**End shake** – The small amount of axle movement in a wheel or balance, vital to its free rotation.

**Escape wheel cock** – A bracket, usually carrying pivot holes for the escape wheel and lever, with one support, as opposed to a bridge, which has two mounting points.

**Fob watch** – This is usually used to describe a small (below 35–40mm in diameter) pocket watch, often intended for use by women.

 **Fourth wheel and pinion** – Between the third wheel and escape wheel, rotates once every sixty seconds. The extended pivot carries the second hand.

**Fusee** – A device that compensates for the decline in torque as the mainspring runs down. It consists of a spiral groove cut into the side of a cone. This is linked via the fusee chain to the barrel. Because of the varying diameter of the fusee, the force acting on the watch train is balanced against the weakening force from the mainspring as it runs down.

 **Fusee chain** – Flexible steel chain (not unlike a miniature modern bicycle chain) used to link the barrel to the fusee.

**Fusee stop iron** – A small spring-loaded lever usually fitted to the underside of the top plate, whose job is to stop the fusee from rotating any more once the watch has been fully wound.

**Gilding** – A thin layer of gold applied to a base metal, usually brass. Gilding was originally done by applying an amalgam of gold and mercury to the metal and then heating it in an open fire, driving off the mercury as a vapour and leaving a thin deposit of gold. This was known as fire gilding and is not to be recommended, as mercury vapour is highly poisonous. During the nineteenth century, this process was replaced by other methods such as gold plating (where gold is deposited using an electrical current), rolled gold or gold filled (where a layer of gold is laminated over a base metal, again usually brass).

**Going barrel** – Because of improvements in the manufacture of steel springs at the beginning of the nineteenth century, it became possible to do away with the fusee and its connecting chain. This meant that the barrel, as it rotates, drives the train directly.

**Great wheel** – The wheel attached to the fusee and via a pinion, drives the centre wheel.

**Half hunter case** – A watchcase with a protective cover over the dial; the centre section of the cover has a watch glass let into it to allow the hands to be viewed so the time can be read without opening the cover. The outside of the front of the cover is sometimes marked with the hours as well. The front cover usually flips open when the pendent button is pressed.

**Hour wheel** – Fits over the cannon pinion and carries the hour hand. The hour wheel completes one revolution every twelve hours.

**Hunter case** – A watchcase design where a metal cover covers the whole of the dial and the cover springs open when the pendant button is pressed.

**Impulse pin (ruby pin)** – The pin on which the fork of the lever acts when imparting energy to the balance.

**Jewelling** – The pivots of the wheels are made to run in jewels that have had small holes drilled through them. This arrangement reduces friction and wear and so the operation of the watch is usually more reliable.

**Lever** – Converts the rotary action of the train to the impulse required to keep the balance oscillating. The lever has a fork at one end, which engages with the impulse jewel on the signal roller. The lever also carries the pallets that receive impulse from the escape wheel.

**Marine chronometer** – This refers to a very accurate type of watch or clock used to measure time at sea with the purpose of determining longitude. John Harrison (1693–1776) designed the first truly accurate watch for this purpose in the 1760s. Later marine chronometers use some variation on the detent escapement.

 **Minute wheel** – Links the cannon pinion and the hour wheel; completes one revolution every sixty minutes.

**Motion work** – An arrangement of wheels and pinions, consisting of the cannon pinion, hour wheel and minute wheel, mounted under the dial, which drives the hands.

**Pallet** – A metal or jewel that protrudes from a part (e.g. balance staff, lever) against which other parts of a watch mechanism act.

 **Pendant** – The part of the watchcase to which the bow is attached. May also carry the pendant button, which, when pressed, flips open either the rear cover or, in half and full-hunter cases, the front cover.

**Pillar** – A length of metal, usually brass, that separates the two movement plates. The pillar is usually riveted to the bottom plate.

**Pinion** – A small-toothed wheel or cog made up of a number of leaves; usually combined with a wheel.

 **Potance** – Can also be spelt 'potence' or 'pottance' – a bracket, mounted on the underside of the top plate that supports the lower balance pivot.

**Ratchet escape wheel and pinion** – The teeth of the escape wheel are designed to alternatively lock and provide impulse to the lever.

**Regulator (index)** – A device that allows the accuracy of a watch to be adjusted by changing the effective length of the balance spring. The longer the balance spring, the slower the watch will run, and the shorter it is, the faster the watch runs. There are several ways in which this can be done; on English fusee lever watches, the regulator is

usually one of three types: Bosley, London Quadrant or mounted on the balance cock.

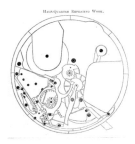

**Repeater** – A watch where the current hour and quarters (and sometimes the minutes) can be sounded at will via a mechanism that strikes on gongs or rods within the watch. The mechanism is activated by pressing a button and can be repeated as often as required, hence the name repeater.

**Rose cutter** – A tool with interchangeable heads designed to cut a flat-bottomed hole of a specific diameter. Can be used to increase the depth of an already cut hole, e.g. adjusting the position of a jewelled pivot.

**Silver gilt** – A way of preventing silver objects from tarnishing by applying a very thin layer of gold over the silver.

**Stop/start work** – An arrangement of levers, usually under the dial, that stops or starts a watch. On most English fusee lever pocket watches, the stop work engages a piece of shaped brass wire with the fourth wheel, escape wheel or edge of table roller.

**Table or single roller** – Where impulse and the safety action are provided by one part. The disc carries both the impulse jewel and the passing crescent to allow the safety pin to pass.

 **Temperature compensation** – A means by which a watch can automatically adjust its rate to compensate for the effect that changes in temperature have on timekeeping.

**Third wheel and pinion** – The wheel between the centre and fourth wheels of the movement.

 **Third-wheel bridge** – A bridge fitted to the bottom plate that carries the lower pivot of the third wheel and fusee. May also carry the lower pivot of the escape wheel.

**Winding square** – The square formed on the end of the fusee arbor, where a key is fitted to wind the watch.

# INDEX

# Related titles from NAG Press

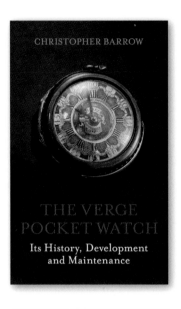

CHRISTOPHER BARROW

THE VERGE
POCKET WATCH

Its History, Development
and Maintenance

CHRISTOPHER BARROW

THE POCKET
WATCH

Restoration, Maintenance
and Repair

New and Revised Edition

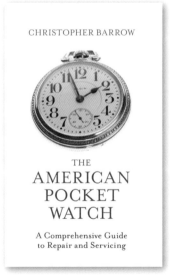

CHRISTOPHER BARROW

THE
AMERICAN
POCKET
WATCH

A Comprehensive Guide
to Repair and Servicing

Practical
Watch
Repairing

Donald de Carle FBHI